Pete —
Thanks for finding
Taylors, they were a hell of a lot
better than the last one.
Dr. John

INFORMATION SECRETS

HEY PETE,
GREAT GRAPHICS
HUH?
WE TOILED
WITH IT AND
IT'S FINALLY HERE.

Pete—
Your help with my
reliability case study
helped to enhance the title
of "subject matter expert" to
an almost believable statement
i.e. you helped me to appear
better than I believed). Does
this make sense? Anyway
thank you so much for
our help & guidance.
Brenda

Pete,
I have really
enjoyed working
for you. I wish
you luck in
upcoming
's.
Daryl

J.D. Thoreson

Dr. J.H.

D0892643

THANKS
FOR All your
HELP & SUPPORT
WITH MY JOB
STATUS
THROUGH THE YEARS,
SINCERELY DAVID ANDREWS

Valuable Information, Ltd.

Richardson, Texas

Pete,
It was fun
challenging & frustrating
but never dull
Best Wishes
Lisa

Published by: Valuable Information, Ltd. Co.
                  Richardson, Texas

Printed in the United States of America

Library of Congress Catalog Card Number: 96-060507

Thoreson, J. D., 1941 -
Blankenship, J. H., 1940 -

Information Secrets / JT, J.D. Thoreson, J.H. Blankenship

ISBN - 0-9643116-3-1

1. Information Valuation
2. Value of Information
3. Information System Value
4. Measuring Information Value
5. Process Valuation
6. Information Measure and Scale

A MYTH BROKEN

For many, the verbal definition of the measurement formulation implies impossibility and creates rigid emotional barriers of hopelessness, useless pursuit or even theological boundary violation. The following scenario suggests how such a thing could happen.

> ## Valuation of Information
>
> The simple measure of information worth is the product of the amount of the goal oriented certainty content (if any) beyond natural **times** the goal reward consequence **plus** the product of the remaining goal **UN**certainty content (if any) **times** the natural equilibrium reward
> —relative to—
> natural equilibrium consequence alone.
>
> JT

The first part of the formulation constitutes the valuable information component and the second part is the natural part. The natural, nonlinear relationships provoke remarkable discontinuities. Higher certainty content increases goal control and reduces natural (random luck) control. Goal reward consequences follow outcome control.

Invisible Barriers. The "upside" of valuable information not only creates exceptional outcome control but often manifests a serendipitous bonus. The combination is both genuine to the holder and awesome to the casual observer. Observers term this the "halo" effect because what they are observing is literally **unnatural good luck**. The definition and quantification of valuable information (above) is the amount of goal control content **beyond natural**. At first encounter the connotation is apparently **supernatural,** bordering on Godlike. The literal meaning of "supernatural" is "beyond nature" or "superior to nature." Such a thing is known to be "impossible." People stop here or shy away from the pursuit.

Permission Granted. In truth valuable information is not at all above nature or superior to it. One can easily see that quantifying information value is well described by the existing laws of nature as we now know them. What it is, is rare, powerful, exceptional, infrequent and elusive. So are most other truly valuable things.

Acknowledgments

This work has been made much less difficult to prepare through the dedicated participation of many. Substantial credit and heartfelt thanks are attributed to:

Pete Kugel	-Editing and Production
William Pratt	-Graphics
Brenda Althoff	-Reliability Engineering
Bonnie Watson	-Editing and Composing
Barbara Cornelius	-Drafting, Editing and Composing
Lisa Rodgers	-Final Preparation

The Value Engineering and Information Engineering teams of 1994, 1995 and 1996 were helpful in the definition of explanation and training aspects of the topics.

Contents

Appendices

Preface

Definitions and bibliography are omitted here in the interest of brevity and in the recognition of the originality. The reader is encouraged to gain access to the series of readings by the authors including The Information Advantage[1], Ahead of Time[2] and Flow of Form.[3]

This book is the computational companion to the series. Fuller and richer discussion is presented in the other works. Pertinent bibliographic references are presented in those works also.

At worst it is the authors' intent to expose the computational path for enumerating information content. At best the reader will be able to conveniently calculate the degree of information content of any object. The difference will likely be in the history of "news" items that the reader has found to be meaningful in the past. As with any activity, practice is important.

---

[1] Thoreson, J.D., The Information Advantage, (1994), Valuable Information Ltd., Richardson, Texas.

[2] Thoreson, J.D., Ahead of Time, (1996), Valuable Information Ltd., Richardson, Texas.

[3] Blankenship, J. H., Flow of Form, (upcoming), Valuable Information Ltd., Richardson, Texas.

1. INTRODUCTION

Information Systems Payoff - How Much? Where?

How much exactly do we get back for what we give in information systems investment? Where are the returns? How does one measure and quantify the magnitude of the returns?

WHY AND WHO NEEDS TO KNOW?

- Chief Executives (CEOs and COOs) beckon because of the need to strengthen the enterprise through wise and prudent investment from preciously short capital.

- Chief Financial Officers and analysts need to know return for proper positioning in the list of resource allocations.

- Chief Information Executives and analysts struggle to serve unlimited information needs from fixed resources without methods to arbitrate highest returns.

- Information Systems Designers need to develop truly valuable information and measure the achievement of same.

- Business Process Specialists observe the apparent linkage between information, systems and processes without measures of the interactions.

- Human Resource Executives and analysts feel that information gained from instruction and training is meaningful but cannot track organizational learning rate without measures.

- Supply Chain Executives and analysts should determine the value of information concerning resource fulfillment.

• Sales, Marketing Executives and analysts need to measure customer, prospect and competition information differences.

• Knowledge Engineers know that information interactions increase knowledge worker performance. How is the content of knowledge gained measured?

Most importantly if one cannot measure and quantify the return of significant investments then it follows that the investment cannot be well directed, well managed or improved. Trial and error is expensive.

If you are in any of the above categories (or have a friend that is), then this book is for you or your friend.

The metrics and measurement and returns from information is a best kept SECRET.

This writing is targeted for high school seniors, undergraduate college students, business analysts, business consultants, performance improvement analysts and personnel with a strong business interest.

One of the reasons for the secret is the relative newness of the Information Age. The subject matter courseware has not been widely available. A second major reason is the fragmentation of pertinent topic disciplines. The requirement is the INTE-GRATION of selected cross discipline topics. We call this Information Engineering.

There are no particularly deep prerequisites except a willingness to study a bit and learn. Since quantification is the objective, expect numbers. A light background in statistics is needed. The reader should be able to calculate simple odds, dice probabilities and the like. Business process understanding is important.

There is no magic. It is really quite simple. Mostly it is just different. People who are rigidly practiced and conditioned to linear, task oriented activities may have difficulty. The Information Advantage video tape offering may be helpful. Some of the sections are deeper and more penetrating than others. Read past the confusing parts and come back to them later.

Information, processes, learning, systems and value are all rather circular by their very nature. Ordering parallel topics in a sequential book is not a convenient presentation.

Structure

This book begins with a potpourri essay on "news" to establish an appreciation for the broad dimensions of the topic. The scope and breadth are very wide at that point.

Next the various topics are addressed with verbal presentation. The core distilled subjects include:

- Enterprise Business Groups
- Processes and Systems
- Measurement
- Value and Valuable Information
- Information Processes

Numerical methods and measures follow the verbal discussions. Small examples are included for illustration. These examples trend toward a three part, comprehensive business setting example. The appendices describe the measure and method of quantifying information system content.

As with any meaningful activity, practice is important. For most, the expectation to immediately put into practice a robust information content measurement system will remain unsatisfied. This is despite the full and complete disclosure of the (quite simple) methodology. Ahead of Time presents the operationalization aspects.

It is the authors' intent that the reader be comforted by the realization that simple and practical method and technique do exist. What was once only imagined is now a doable thing. Given reader interest in the subject we hope to clarify for you what needs to be worked on next.

Information content messages arrive in time-spaced parcels, packages, bits, pieces and streams. Thus, we need to address fractional information, accumulations of fractions and differences. In fact, we will get very close to defining where fractions themselves come from and what they mean.

For the technique to be understood, applied and trusted we expect that the reader will desire insight into the origin and application of information content. That is the purpose of the other books. This work is about **information content measurement**. At the risk of creating more confusion than clarity the first several chapters do attempt to introduce and/or refresh the topics. An otherwise simple computational technique may become cluttered in the detail of the example or unfamiliarity with the example.

Information conveyance deals not with one single object but multiples. There is never one. The notion of senders and receivers, audiences, broadcast to multiples and the like is fundamental. Children remark, "Ha! Ha! I have information that you don't." Groups, corporations and nations often behave the same.

The second fundamental notion about information is the organization of it. Random cannot be organized but everything else can be. The organizational aspects bring in the secret part. All energy comes in two parts. One part is the part that we have often studied. The other part is the organizational part.

Can the light from the sun ignite a piece of paper? Yes, it can with the aid of an inanimate magnifying glass. No energy is added. The existing energy is reorganized and redirected. It is this peculiar, subtle and powerful aspect of organized energy that we speak.

The center of focus for the measures and metrics resides at the topic of effective control and/or the lack of effective control. "Effect" means that the measure is taken at the impact point(s) as opposed to the alternatives. It would be good for the reader to keep in mind throughout the material the notion of hard and soft **control systems**.

The Secret is Kept

Information content calculation, valuable information determination, and information valuation are best kept **secrets by choice**. Nowhere are the rigorous characteristics of "valuable information" defined.

Business schools **choose** not to inform their students of the basic mathematical and natural science skills necessary to construct and perform the rather simple information valuation computations. A very few hours of curriculum would be sufficient. The absence of these few hours is **blinding**.

Engineering develops the appropriate mathematical and scientific skills in students, but it **chooses** to defocus interest away from business and/or information engineering. The absence of interest is **blinding**.

Statisticians **choose** to eliminate and forget the unit labels that go along with their probability ratios. Worse yet, the mechanical formation of informational groupings disguises and hides information.

Sociologists and psychologists **choose** to discount information impact. Instead, these disciplines **choose** to describe information conditioning as emotion.

As a consequence of the sum of these **choices**, information understanding and apprciation resides in a needless void. The secret is kept by a bit of collective ignorance.

2. INFORMATION PROCESSES

AN ESSAY

News - Short for New Things

Here is a news flash. We cannot individually or collectively break the laws of nature. That is not news. All are bound by the natural laws and born into a world where nature's laws are dictatorial. For example, gravity was in evidence before each person's conception and for every moment since. That is not news. That is familiarity. Gravity is so familiar it is invisible. So what law(s) of science dictate news? If something as powerful as gravity is invisible, what else might be? What is the science upon which **news happens** and **secrets are suppressed**?

Who Cares?

The United States Constitution founders thought it necessary to cite information and news, specifically freedom of communication. Businesses expend considerable resource and consume precious capital to collect and publish news about profit. Consequences result. Stuff happens. The rumor mill and task groups exchange hot news items. News seems to be the "force" in task force. Energy and resource are consumed and consequences result. Advertising and media firms make a living from collecting and distributing news. There is obvious economic gain from the activity. Money exchange is a consequence. News is important! Why?

In the brief previous passage we have sketched a thing that consumes time, resource, investment and is important enough to have a place in the constitution. Various forms of news create wealth and cause consequences. Yet few know the science. Who cares? A few do, more should.

Why?

Because if one knows and others don't and the item is **consequential** — then the payoff advantage goes toward the informed, if it can be **actionable** and **monetized**. This book develops **MEASURES** for **INFORMATION CONTENT** and the **UTILITY of INFORMATION.**

The Science and Philosophy of News

The science of news works like "20 Questions" in combination with **truth** or **consequences**. The application deals with any two or more objects. People and groups of people are a most interesting application. People, collected for the purpose of economic enterprise, are the focus here.

News and the science of information start with differences (and end with differences). No two people can be identical. People cannot simultaneously occupy the same physical space, period. At birth the empty reservoir of knowledge begins receiving information through the senses. The first and forever continuous personal bombardment of information is from the voice, touch and feel of nature's laws. So too must corporations gather information from their birth. Whether studied formally or not, people "learn" to obey nature's (science's) rules. All people must obey because one cannot escape the truth of the real laws (gravity) whatever these laws really, really are. Nature does not require a police force to administer the laws (science does). Nature's laws are fair, equal opportunity, unbiased and strict. Those that cannot or will not learn or learn fast enough are treated harshly. They disappear to the netherworld. The same is true for enterprises and people. So does their influence. The resulting set of people hold in common that their ancestry learned, perhaps believed but certainly avoided any early catastrophic encounter with nature's penalties (they survived at least through the puberty and reproductive cycle). So at this point people (1) cannot occupy the same space at the same time and (2) hold the laws of nature truthful and rigid (even if one doesn't know exactly what they are).

The scale ranging from **uniqueness** to **commonality** is going to be an important ingredient to our measure later.

Now comes science — social science and natural science. Scientists interpret and communicate nature's apparent laws. Parents are the first science teachers — usually mothers.

Then come professional teachers who reinterpret mom's laws. The reservoir now begins to encounter peculiar **discontinuities**. For the next 10 to 25 years, differing interpretations happen all over the place.

Notice that this format is a type of distributed system. The point here is that everyone's experience is unique because of the accumulation of sensory experiences gained through just regular old living life . . . news events. These news events have filled in something that was previously missing. This is not only a United States phenomena, it takes place around the globe.

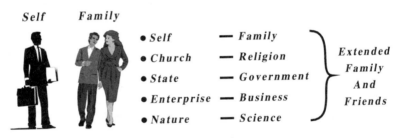

Self   *Family*

- *Self* — *Family*
- *Church* — *Religion*
- *State* — *Government*   *Extended Family And Friends*
- *Enterprise* — *Business*
- *Nature* — *Science*

One of the **timeless** constants is the stress and friction between contending **control processes**. For example, a fundamental dynamic conflict arises between the ideal of **freedom** and the necessity for **order** in relation to **goal** definition and achievement. Each group, through rules, establishes goal doctrine and communicates prolific volumes of symbolic data espousing the respective goal system. As our objective is the stable quantification measures for information content, the choice of tools for the task is science based. State and enterprise are not stable forms and church does not rigorously pursue arithmetic symbols as the basis of founding doctrine.

The Name of the Thing is Not the Thing

Information processes are much more prevalent than most appreciate. The symbolic tags given tend to disguise their underlying structure. Below are listed a few of the renamed information processes. Appreciate that this "labeling" establishes the context expectation of the information content from each.

News	-	Information
Education and Training	-	Subject matter information
Consulting	-	Information exchange
Publishing; All Media	-	Information exchange
Accounting	-	Information exchange
Advertising	-	Information exchange
Diagnostic Physicians	-	Information exchange
Policy Management	-	Information - Rules
Government	-	Information - Rules
Task Forces	-	Information exchange - actions
Committees, Priorities, Allocations	-	Information-action-allocation
All Religions	-	Informational
All Mathematics	-	Informational
All Art	-	Informational
All Music	-	Informational
All Libraries	-	Informational
All Engineering	-	Informational
All Management & Coordination	-	Informational
All Money	-	Informational
All Conversations	-	Informational
All Process Structure & Sequence	-	Informational

(and so on . . . . .)

The list goes very far onward. Discounting information is not wise. These processes require investment and capital consumption. The same processes are wealth generators.

Here is some "news" — there is a winning strategy among the chaos. The winners consistently operate above normal. The distribution of winners is skewed away from normal. They are simply **not normal**.

Pervasive - How Big Can It Get?

Our earlier book, <u>The Information Advantage</u>, states that anything that makes a difference is an information candidate. It is literally true that all information comes from **pattern varia-tions**. However, not all data are meaningful information. A spot of ink forming a letter or word on an otherwise blank page makes a difference and therefore constitutes data and a poten-tial for information. It may not "mean" anything to us, but it is a difference. Musical notes in a tune make a difference. The time between notes makes a difference. All patterns, all forms, the edges of things, night versus day, all wave forms, all objects are information candidates. When and if these event objects become the cause of a consequential difference, information happens.[4] When the information provokes a goal gain it is valuable.

Literally everything in the universe is difference information. Information is the most pervasive thing in the universe. Some of it is a lot more meaningful and valuable. Information that provokes a high goal gain outcome is valuable.

The differences are classified as differences in "kind" and differences in "degree." The previous list illustrated differ-ences of kind. Next we will show differences in degree (mag-nitude, quantity and intensity).

---

[4]   See discussion of "Information Moment" in <u>The Information Advantage</u>, pp. 3-5.

The Information Advantage is illustrated with many patterns of difference. For example:

Do you see a triangle?

We sense the triangle because of the edges of the form. Removing the circles would yield a blank piece of paper which could have hundreds of invisible (to us) triangles — or none at all. Differences occur that we cannot sense. The electric light is blinking sixty times a second. Just like the invisible triangles, the blinks are invisible to us. This does not mean they cannot be measured by instruments. Each symbol and each object absorbs and or reflects a different energy level as it is illuminated by the light bulb or other radiation. Everything is oscillating and causing waves. Sound waves, sight waves, touch waves, smell waves, energy waves. The source of waves is energy, waves are change cycles and are also information. The duality between the waves, the cause of the waves and the form of the waves are topics we intend to clarify. Entropy laws describe the energy flow and variation transforms, causing information. It should not be surprising that variation (variance) in statistics is linked to entropy in energy and patterns of difference that we call information. In The Information Advantage, Thoreson describes the unification among the relationships of information, entropy and change. In business, customers are only attracted to something different because it will take something different from what they have to make a difference they desire to pay for.

The reader may gain insight in regard to thinking about the concept of differences through exposure to eastern cultures. Westerners are taught to embrace good and reject evil by the church. Schools teach recognition of true and false. Government expects obeyance of the lawful right and avoidance of the unlawful wrong.

In Eastern thinking everything contains its opposite and **depends** on its opposite for meaning.

The measuring and evaluation system we are constructing here is similar to the Eastern concept of difference.

Yin/Yang

A regulator or governor of some sort is required to measure and balance the goodness gains versus the energy expended. Nature provides the governor. The Second Law of Energy (thermodynamics) is the primary subject here. It deals with the natural rules of how energy flows and does not flow from one form to another. The information particular feature deals with rules of change, transformation and variation. The whole thing should not be more difficult than the following example.

The Arithmetic of News

"There is very little chance of rain." All understand what is meant by much chance and little chance. It relates to the amount of probability attached to any given event.

So when we are asked what chance, we may observe, inspect and assess that there is much chance or little. We may go even further and establish in our own minds a scale of expressions establishing different degrees in some such way as follows.

> It is certain not to rain.
> > It is very unlikely to rain.
> > > It is unlikely to rain.
> > > > It is likely to rain as not.
> > > It is likely to rain.
> > It is very likely to rain.
> It is certain to rain.

These expressions **except** the first, fourth and last are vague and indefinite. This vagueness is of little consequence because in most cases it is not possible to make an accurate estimate.

But there are other classes of events in which partial knowledge is present that do permit us to describe quite exactly the amount of certainty and by the alternate side, ignorance. Probability always implies some ignorance on the party entertaining the expectation. Probability attached to any event depends on the degree of this ignorance or doubt. The omniscient person has no doubt and therefore probability does not apply (or does it?).

This is where news comes in. The very same event will be **unequally** probable to different people whose previous news of the circumstances relating to the event is different.

For instance, suppose a friend sets out on a cruise with five other passengers on a ship with thirty crew members. We receive the news that **a person** has fallen overboard and drowned. So long as the news is confined to the fact that one individual among the thirty-six on board has been lost, the probability of our friend is small. The odds are said to be thirty-five to one against it being our friend.

If, however, a next news message arrives that augments our knowledge by indicating that a **passenger** was the one lost, the odds have changed. The odds are now only five to one against it being our friend. The news changed the odds at **our end**.

Given that the event really happened it has already been determined whether it was our friend or not. The probability expresses what amount of pertinent information we have **received** relative to the event. The news is changing the probability from our prospective but does not change a past event.

A general rule may be seen to be evolving here. We know that the ratio of possible outcomes to possibilities will lie between the limits of zero and unity. If we assume that all values between these limits are equally likely, we are establishing a condition which connotes "entirely or arbitrarily unknown." Everybody knows this much. Information content exceptions occur beyond this baseline. As we begin quantifying information content the definition is extended. Information is anything that makes a difference from the starting **basis** of invisible, random, uniform, equal, familiar or normal. It is against this basis that we measure the news content.

3. ENTERPRISE GROUPS, GROUPWARE, COLLECTIONS OF WORKGROUPS, ENSEMBLES OF RESOURCES

Workgroups – Worknets, Committees and Task Forces

Our "best practice" search has uncovered others that have pointed to the fantastic power of collaborative network personal (as in mental) computing. The power of this phenomena is not new. Plato, Aristotle, Chinese researchers, John von Neumann and Alan Turing, among many others, recognized its existence. The term "Worknets" is reputed to have been coined by Michael Schrange, a researcher at MIT, journalist for the Los Angeles Times, Wall Street Journal, Boston Globe and author ("Shared Minds," 1962). Worknets, Successsnets, Businets and Profitnets are **closely** related. The idea is that certain compositions of **properly focused** ordinary people connect with each other to create **extraordinary** value. The difficulty is one of defining the characteristics so that the power could be reproduced in a reliable manner. We shall show here how that is possible, how it happens and how to quantify the topic.

The bottom line of our experience points to essential requirements for designing precise networks of competencies linked inside and outside the enterprise. The performance of small and medium sized groups holds the key to value building in an enterprise. Groups in this context are not restricted to unitized (or functional) groups. A single person may be in many groups other than the physically assigned unit. It is a network of like-minded peers. The sharing of expertise, the collaboration, the synergy of high value information is contagious and is a best practice. When like-minded bumps into contrary-minded, a thing called entropy happens. Two contending belief systems attempt to convey "truth" to the other. Entropy is a Greek term meaning transform. Each group is attempting to transform the other.

High value creation groups find, choose and operate to exemplary practice criteria that result in exceptional price/performance results. This synergy is not accomplished with silicon computers alone. Rather extraordinary performances occur as a properly guided common consequence of workgroup communications. The core determinant of success is developing and harnessing the information processes to advantage. Groupware is not so much a technology based importance as a **process based** importance. Loosely and tightly bound groups are the way in which work gets **done**. The coordination of getting work done always requires information processes. The investment or consumption of energy or capital cannot be avoided, although it can be minimized.

Investment can be **aimed** and **targeted**. Aimed, targeted (organized) energy is more **powerful**. Focusing energy intensifies its consequence. There is a cost in coordinating collective work activity. This cost is not an item on the general ledger. . . yet.

Groupware, coordination of work and building high value creation groups are going to be increasingly critical to enterprise success and survival. Examples of organizational form include PepsiCo's "inverted pyramid," Charles Handy's "shamrock organization," Eastman Chemicals' "pizza organizational model," the "horizontal organization" and the "virtual organization." Fundamentally what is being restructured is group information flow dynamics and peculiar forms of asset structures. The experiments to restructure organizational shapes are illustrations of investment searching for better information connection processes. Why is that news? They are experimenting and guessing rather than designing.

Organization structures, task forces, committees and similar group structures, including those encouraged by the Quality doctrines, can work. Because the investment is high it is good to deeply understand how and why. The lack of understanding causes waste and high failure rates. Ad hoc task forces, group systems, and organizational changes create random results similar to rain dances and witchcraft. A few times it rains after the dance. All of a sudden everyone is doing it. The mathematics of success in teaching task forces, committees (particularly the finance committee), Quality groups, consulting and workgroups follow energy and reliability laws (Refer to the example, pages 29, 133-157). The probability of improving the "goodness" of the result over the individual solution "goodness" improves with additional people.

Simply put, the information is better with two collaborating than either separately. Three improves over two and so on. Believe it or not there is mathematics here!

Does this mean that four "topic ignorant" people can create a better solution than one topic smart and one "topic ignorant" person? No — probably not — very small chance. It means that four "topic ignorant" people can develop a better solution by combined focus than any one of them can do on their own. The term "topic ignorant" is not intended to be derogatory. It only means that the person is not accomplished at the particular topic in question. It means uninformed, unpracticed in the **topic**.

Collaborative groupware means that there is a certain amount of <u>collective</u> news exchanged that can be focused and directed so that the shared knowledge approach and resulting solution can be superior to the individual solution which would have resulted from each. Notice that there is no free lunch. The energy laws rule out something for nothing. Perpetual motion is not in the cards. The energy (cost) is increasing from the multiple participants. Where is the payoff?

What we intend to show is exactly equivalent to the way that a magnifying lens focuses the sun's rays to ignite a piece of wood or paper. The power of the rays is intensified not ten percent but hundreds and thousands of percent.

The following is an illustration of workgroup information content improvement. The people in this example are informed to varying degrees on the topic in question.

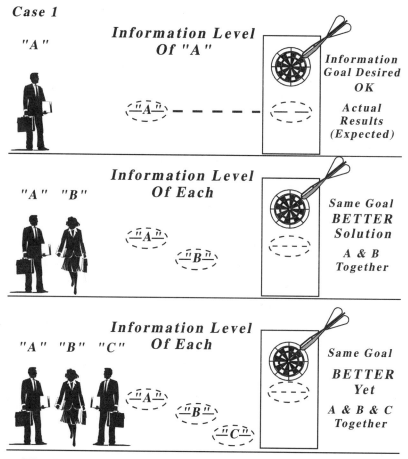

Case 1

"*A*"

Information Level Of "A"

Information Goal Desired OK

Actual Results (Expected)

"*A*" "*B*"

Information Level Of Each

Same Goal BETTER Solution A & B Together

"*A*" "*B*" "*C*"

Information Level Of Each

Same Goal BETTER Yet A & B & C Together

The Higher Collaboration, The Better The Solution.
Solution Goodness: $A \leq A+B \leq A+B+C$

The probability that the collective group information contributes to a superior solution is greater than each individually. This should not be a surprise.

The feature that differentiates humans from all others is the ability to communicate information toward collective action.

The power is magnified in a very peculiar and interesting way. ADDITIONS MULTIPLY!! Think about this! Powerful leverage occurs when the **addition** of one object **multiplies** others.

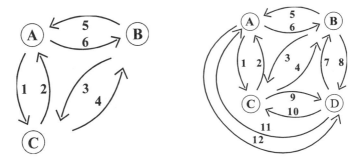

This very interesting scenario demonstrates the interactions that can and do occur if properly channeled. Notice that the addition of one new member "D" multiplies the exchange linkages from six (6) possibilities to twelve (12). This is both good news and bad news. If the activity is value focused then there is a **value multiplier**. This is good. But the **cost** has **multiplied** also. Not good. This is one of the governors. Group relationships require increasingly higher maintenance.

Recall those topic ignorant people earlier. Add a subject matter knowledgeable person (expert) to the group. Focus on a particular subject together with a reward/penalty incentive operating (a scorecard). Give identity labels to the integrated scenario. Call it a classroom with student participants and an instructor. What results is a "news system" called education. To the students the events are new (news).

The information flows from instructor to students and among the students. The students improve their capacity for good performance on the subject. Students are more **certain** and less **uncertain**. On the surface the students get topic-wise smarter (less ignorant) but the instructor does not get "dumber." (Often, in fact, the instructor gains a bit from the students.) The subject matter is "distributed" in a sense from the news source (the instructor) to the students (recipients). An interesting exchange happens. Before the learning event the instructor knew and the students didn't. After the exchange event the instructor still knows and so do the students (given that they learned). Instructing, training, practicing and consulting are forms of **information processes**. Nothing else is being "delivered."

An excellent and high consequence, every day life illustration of exactly these group decision scenarios can be found in the American jury system. A group of twelve people are collected to listen to evidence and render a consequential verdict. The **outcome** of the process is a guilty or not **choice**. The jury choice reaches a finality of certainty in the dispute. One can perhaps appreciate the difference in outcome if the jury verdict rules were changed from unanimous toward majority. The amount of certainty in the outcomes would be different. The degree or amount of information content required to reach a guilty verdict would be reduced. It should also be clear as to how information during jury selection biases the composition of the jury which in turn biases the outcome. Even prior to the selection of specific jurors the decision on whether to include jury candidates on the basis of drivers license or property ownership causes large differences in the outcomes. Courtroom evidence is not the only information in the process which determines the outcomes!!

OOPS - Another Downside - Truth is Present

Churchill once said, "Some people stumble over the truth, get up and go on as if nothing had happened."

One might think about the similarity to the way that democracy works. Let's all vote! The consensus solution is the "best" solution. This is not quite the case. The consensus is not good or correct or optimal any more than when everyone agreed that the world was FLAT. Columbus capitalized by knowing differently. What does happen with consensus is the discovery of a path on which the consenting participants are willing to expend collective energy. Later we will define valuable information. Valuable is often the antithesis of consensus. However, consensus is always well founded as a groupware model because the result may very well be the "best" next step forward that can be accomplished.

The reader will notice the following case is very similar in structure but rather opposite in outcome. The addition of one member that "knows" the truth changes the situation, but not as much as we would perhaps like.

Here is a visual view of such a case:

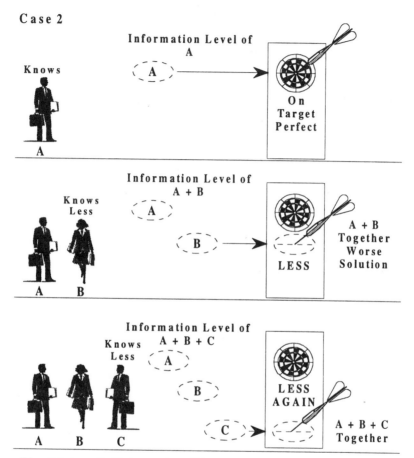

Case 2

The Higher Collaboration, The More Average The Solution.
Solution Goodness: $A \geq A+B \geq A+B+C$

What happened? In the previous case the solution got better.
Now it is getting worse.

In Case 2 the solution is actually compromised downward. The consensus is perhaps "B." The truth is exposed but cannot be "accepted" because the best experience (previous news) of "B" cannot quite stretch to "A" and "C" cannot stretch to "B". "A" in essence gets out voted. The "best" group solution is thus downgraded by consensus. The best that the "A" person can do is say, "I told you so." This case is akin to the Columbus scenario.

The first case considered the situation where the goal is a "stretch." None of the members "knows" or possesses the exactly precise, absolutely correct answers. The example might be the choosing of policies to harmoniously conduct a large group, enterprise or nation. The solution improved.

The second case is termed the "**I told you so**" case. This case is one where the actually true optimum solution is present . . . but unrecognized.

Here is a difference. In the second case, the amount of best subject matter "goodness" information did not change relative to truth, but the average did. The laws of relativity, probability and energy are ever present. The fact that students now know more of what the instructor knows is good and significant. The fact also remains that the same degree of uncertainty still exists if analyzed on the basis of the "best" combined solution versus the really, really, real optimum. Nothing much "new" happened (to the instructor).

In a sense, the instructor did experience lost opportunity by expending energy to elevate the students' knowledge versus expending the equivalent energy elevating his/her personal subject matter knowledge level. The instructor could have been stretching UPWARD, collaborating with higher knowledge masters, rather than DOWNWARD with students. We owe a large thanks for the teachers' willingness to teach.

Reliability and Information are Related

The analysis and thinking about these two cases relates to the study of **reliability**. The average group performance reliability in the topic increased in both cases. Properly configured redundancy (topic focused) always improves the reliability of the outcome as opposed to what would have happened if each member had attempted the solution individually and summed the collective outputs. If average is used as a measure then the information content of both group cases can be said to have improved. However, if "best" is used as the measure then there was little or no improvement in the second case. Best did not get better in the second case. Refer to Appendix A for a "measures" brief.

Information analysis and reliability analysis are tightly coupled. Both deal with controlling the odds of future success and failure. Both topics involve the prudent **investment** at one point **in time** to influence **outcomes** at later points **in time**. Both involve the control of dynamic, probabilistic processes. Reliability engineering, information engineering, and, to a lesser extent, value engineering are all linked.

The information scale and measure which we shall build here takes on important characteristics of reliability. The higher the reliability, the lower the failure rate. Perfect reliability would yield 100 percent success and no failure. The perfect instructor, "I told you so" case is thus resolved. Valuable information works the same. Better information yields more success and less failure.

Particular Particulars

The evidence of (and the true) information content is simply the reliability of getting a "particular particular" correct. Repeated success is information evidence. Failing a trial is evidence of uncertainty and is variance and is anti-information.

Later we will point out important semantic and practice differences relating to **reliability** as interpreted and practiced in the
accounting profession.

If we were to bring in more and more people into the previous
case examples and were able to diagram the results, a normal
distribution would be the likely outcome.

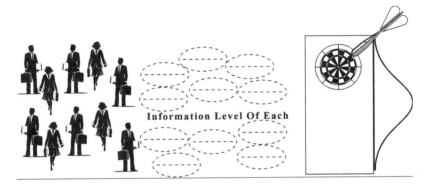

Information Level Of Each

Most people have been exposed to the "bell shaped curve."

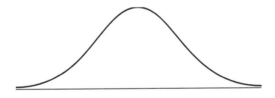

It is often called the normal distribution. This name is quite
good because it symbolically represents one of the prominent
configurations in which nature manufactures things. This
distribution is nature's normal production pattern.

One might recall the "curve" grading system used in schools.
SAT or Iowa Basic Skills standard is the appropriate "bench-
mark" context with students rather than the floating competitive curve.

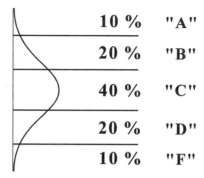

10 %	"A"
20 %	"B"
40 %	"C"
20 %	"D"
10 %	"F"

The competitive context of the normal distribution is consequential. Consider the skill set and competency content in a
high incentive good topic of an enterprise where the "F's"
cancel out the "A's", the "D's" cancel the "B's" and what
remains is a corporation that is really average, a "C".

If a corporation or a group possesses average "C" information
then it is vulnerable to enterprises consisting of only the "A"
and "B" exemplars. This is shown in the following diagram.
The left case is the normal enterprises IQ, the right side is
higher GPA[5]. Something is present in the exemplars that is
missing with the average.

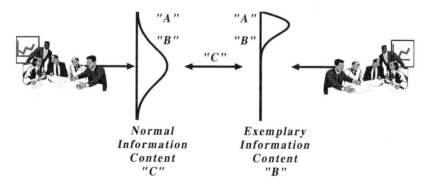

*Normal
Information
Content
"C"*

*Exemplary
Information
Content
"B"*

---

[5]   GPA in this context means Greater Performance Aptitude in critical business topics.

Given that the content is related to particular particulars, the business resultant yields the POWER to compete in the market place. The exemplary enterprise competes favorably with the average. It simply competes on the basis of possessing superior information from which to choose paths of investment that will return greater rewards. The remainder of this book further explains some of the formulative prerequisites. There is no magic. It is simply knowing when and where to invest energy.

The power computation for a corporation's economic information engine is analogous and calculated similarly to horsepower of an automobile engine. In this sense a 500 horsepower engine does not always guarantee beating a 300 horsepower engine. The odds, however, favor the more powerful. For those that do not possess a Ph.D., have hope. Valuable information and courseware inflicted on most students are not the same. The topics most instructed often are not particularly valuable.

For those readers that have a compelling need to monetize information power do not fret. The calculation or estimation of the economic consequence can be accomplished. This scenario is presented later and again in the appendices.

Measurement Patterns of All Processes

Fortunately **all** processes behave in a similar pattern, including information processes. This diagram shows the commonality among processes.

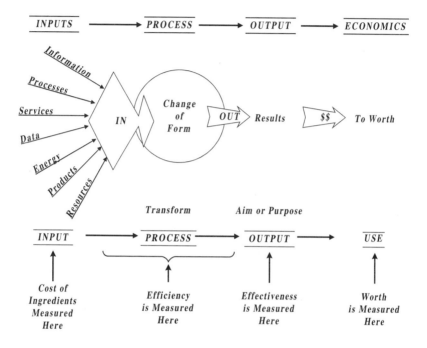

The measurement "point" will be critical to the measured result. It is good to keep this diagram in mind. It will be used several times. The resulting measure is conditioned by **where** as much as **how** the measure is constructed.

Measure and the act of measuring carries along with it obligations to make measure **distinct** from synthesis, thinking, philosophy and conjecture. Here is the key to the distinction. Proper measurement must consist of data that arises from consuming energy, however small or large, from the object being measured. This is not a harsh constraint.

The importance is in determining which object, exactly, is being measured. The measurement distinction requires that there are actualized observations or instruments **connected** to the object in some manner.

One might summarize this measuring foundation by stating that the evidence comes from the source.

Finding the Fault and Cause of Success

The traditional practice of process control carries with it the implied doctrine of searching for the faults in the system . . . the errors. The doctrine specifies that, among other things, there are two sources of error: random and systematic. Systematic sources of variation produce errors that have an assignable cause and introduce a particular bias. Random sources of variation produce errors that, due to a multiplicity of causes, can neither be observed nor controlled. The technique described here measures both.

The control chart is based on the premise that all processes create a discernible **pattern** in the output. Upon repeated measurement the frequency distribution of a given dimension might be expected to fall between two (evidently) limiting values called "exception limits."

The control chart is an **attention focusing** mechanism. It selectively presents the analyst with those "exceptional" situations that require attention.

When the dimension falls outside the defined limits (i.e., an "out-of-control" situation is encountered), there is a high probability that the event is due to a systemic condition for which we can try to find an assignable cause. The latency effect of informational bias is troubling because the information event (learning) may have occurred long ago and is just now being used.

We submit that with proper alteration and best practice thinking, the very same mechanism can be dispatched to find the **fault of success.**[6] Attention in this case is dispatched to find the cause of positive outcomes rather than negative. Before fixing what is "thought" to be wrong one needs to know what is right . . . for certain!

The emphasis here is to choose a measure and measuring point that includes BOTH success and failure. Preoccupation with failure analysis finds much of it to the exclusion of success measurement. Efficiency indoctrinates failure-only thinking.

It is necessary to choose a dimension of consequence to monitor (this is true also in traditional processes). Further, it is a requirement that the dimension must relate to the process aim or output such that effectiveness is being measured and monitored. Finally, the dimension must be constructed in a manner which is "two sided." This means that numerical movement in one direction (say up) is goal attainment good and in the opposite direction is not. In business such dimensions include net income before tax (profit) or revenue divided by investment and/or marketshare. Uncertainty is the measure of information deficiency.

Process control then becomes the matter of controlling or biasing the guidance statistic ever upward (positive goal good). Given the measures mentioned above the notion of controlling profitability upward arises as a control aim or objective. Attention and effort similar in nature to success variance is devoted to finding whose fault it is that profit happens! Such activity is an important ingredient in value delivery analysis.

---

[6]   The Information Advantage, op. cit., p. 218, presents two "alarms." Only one is
    attended. The other is the "success" alarm.

The fault, when identified, will not be personal. It will be found in superior collective information processes and practices (See "Control is the Key," page 120).[7]

The descriptive view which we prefer is that of the enterprise economic engine. The reason for this view is several fold. First, the term incorporates the essential ingredients of the man-machine integrated organization. Second, all the analytical methods of science, engineering, process management and economics are available for use. Third, a consistent aim is most likely to exist. Finally, optimization must address the whole as well as the decomposed parts.

Many people, groups and enterprises learn to capitalize on "I told you so" information differences. We have often used the Rothschild "Waterloo Story" as a vivid illustration (refer to companion video). Rothschild, in effect, amassed a considerable fortune by selling, "I told you so" information to **doubters**.

---

[7]   "Very Best Business Practices" 1996, Article Internet Web publication, Valuable Information, Inc. Ahead of Time treats the subject extensively to the point of disclosing information based, enterprise optimization.

4. PROCESSES,
INFORMATION PROCESSES,
UNCERTAINTY REDUCTION PROCESSES
AND INFORMATION DELIVERY

Processes:[8] Requirements and Review

A strict definition of process (or system) must include three
elements. For something to be a process it must:

1. Possess an aim or **goal**.
2. Accomplish some **change** in the **form** or state of the
   inputs to the intended resulting **outputs**.
3. Create the necessary and sufficient data to improve itself
   (wellness, illness).

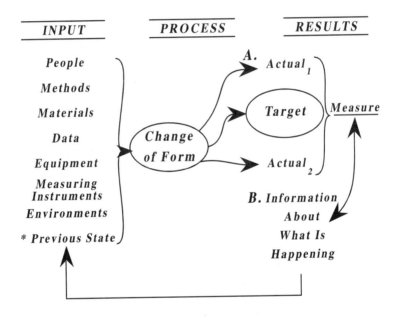

The idea of process now has a circular dynamic flow about it
from the viewpoint of the information. The measuring instruments feed back the data prerequisite to correct or control the
process. Goal and feedback are very familiar to process
engineers.

---

8   Process, Systems and Practices are used synonymously throughout this text.

An example may help here.

Say that the aim of a manufacturing process is the construction of a tractor. The input ingredients are assembled for the tractor recipe and into the process they go. The diagram below is a view of the expected future results versus what actually happened.

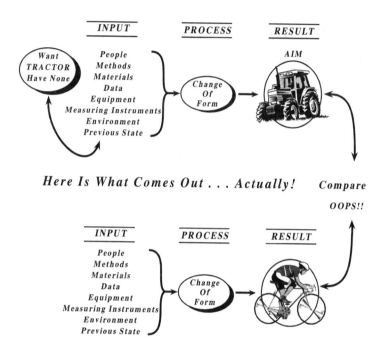

The resulting bicycle is not all bad, but it was not the intended aim.

When the measurement instruments compare the goal of the
tractor to the actual of a bicycle there is a difference . . . variation. A message about this observation is sent back to the input
of the process suggesting that perhaps new ingredients or
process steps might be adopted.

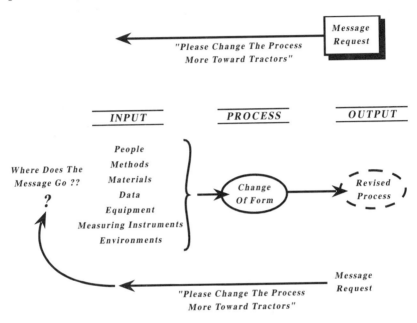

Yet another problem arises. There is no input that matches
"process" for the message request to match. The old process
needs to be an input and mixed with the other ingredients so
that a revised "closer to tractor" process can be enacted.

Completeness

Consider reclassifying the inputs into a complete but still simple and small list. The following is offered as a candidate list. The graphic also depicts a historical measurement scale difficulty in terms of the "amount of" the item or the "worth" of the item.

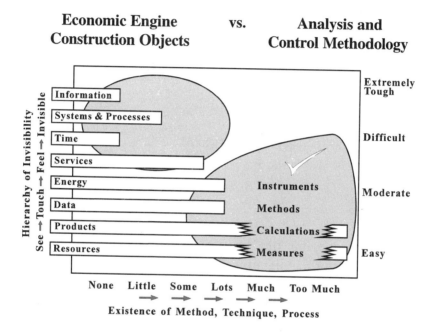

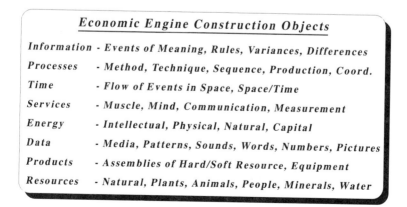

Economic Engine Construction Objects

Information	- Events of Meaning, Rules, Variances, Differences
Processes	- Method, Technique, Sequence, Production, Coord.
Time	- Flow of Events in Space, Space/Time
Services	- Muscle, Mind, Communication, Measurement
Energy	- Intellectual, Physical, Natural, Capital
Data	- Media, Patterns, Sounds, Words, Numbers, Pictures
Products	- Assemblies of Hard/Soft Resource, Equipment
Resources	- Natural, Plants, Animals, People, Minerals, Water

Now an updated process model is available to us. Here is the new view.

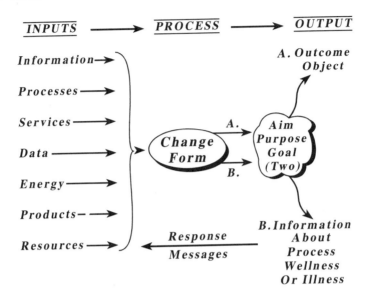

Some processes are recursive or adaptable. In the case of the tractor example, the "old" process needs to be an **input** so that a revised tractor making process can be the **output**.

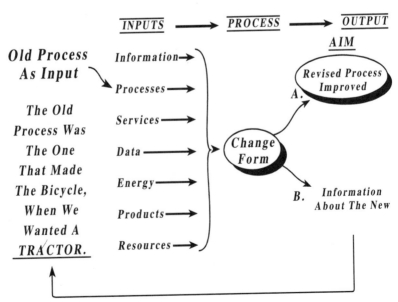

This model permits us to accomplish more of the things we know we are doing but were unable to specify with the other model, for example, process reengineering. In this model we can input an old process and aim to create a result of a new process.

The depiction in the above figure is a process to change process. In business this is the process to reengineer processes. In people this **process biases** subsequent actions and is termed **"learning."**

Temporal Plane

However, in our very discussing of this we added a new thing. We added the concept of past-present-future. This happened when we said we were **going to create** an improved process from the old process. It occurs that the inputs to the process need to be able to include PROSPECTIVE views. This is not surprising. When we aimed to make a tractor, that, in fact, was a future event. The designs of new things are <u>prospective</u>. A new input includes the design of future things and stuff. We need time.

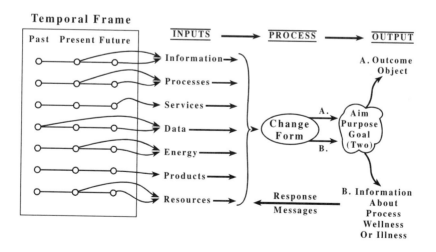

To complete our model we should add a time frame positioning for each of the input possibilities. We can now input past, present and/or future systems, processes, services, products, resources and everything!

Now, we can input, for example, our old experience of the prospective tractor, the past result (bicycle), the request (present), the old process (past), and the (future) design of process improvements. The chances improve of achieving our aim of creating a tractor.

Scale of Application - The Boundaries

It would be good now to test the range of process possibilities for which this model can apply. Let us do a simple thing, a medium thing, and a really big thing.

A Simple Thing

Let us take the process of a simple thing like adding "1 + 1" to equal "2".

The aim of the process is to correctly perform the addition of two symbols to create a resultant. The method or process of choice is selected from past success in performing such activities. The items of input are the two "1s" and those two objects are acted upon with the addition method to become a resultant outcome of "2".

The resulting "2" is compared to other alternatives and judged to be correct. There is no variance.

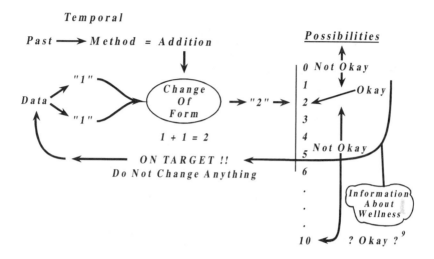

This worked out great. The small simple processes fit the model. Let us step to something of larger scale. How about a new customer offering . . . a new product.

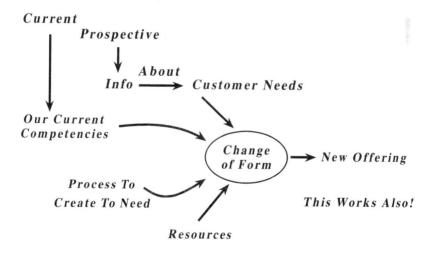

This example is equivalent to the tractor previously illustrated.

---

[9]   A change in numbering systems base would make 10 correct to the base 2.

A Medium Thing

Consider the task that many enterprises face of ENTERPRISE reengineering. The aim of the process would likely be to increase the competitiveness as evidenced by the resulting measurement of market share, profit and growth. The subject process to be reengineered in such an activity is the value delivery process.

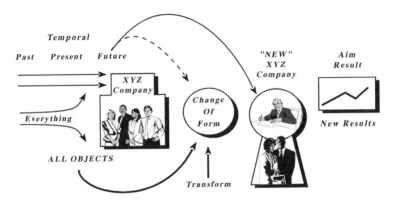

The future view of the resulting new revised enterprise becomes an input along with all resources, products, processes, systems, policy, capital structure, and so on. The old enterprise recipe is remolded with freshened everything that matters. The result is a new XYZ with a higher state of competitiveness. The later example (page 133) shows how this transformation can happen.

Comment. Recall that the focus here is measurement of information content. The point is that the design of measurement criteria must **span** these wide ranges of possibilities. We started with the invisible triangles and now we are at the enterprise level. The next step is national. There is a cascading set of metrics.

Large Things

A large thing might be to reengineer the wellness of a nation or even of a collection of nations. This is the scale at which Deming SUCCESSFULLY applied process.

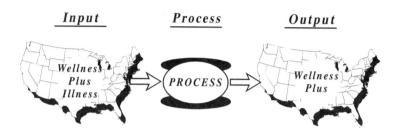

Such is the power of properly applied process thinking and doing.

A few pages from now we hope to show EXACTLY what composes and comprises processes. The reader may want to recall or review these previous **scales** and sizes of processes.

Process Potency - Information Process

There should not have been much "new" in the previous review except for perhaps the measurement points. We have been dealing with physical space for the most part. Where we are going next is **different**. Information space is quite different. The presentation is NOT exactly feedback as has been traditionally presented to this point. We are now entering advanced CYBERspace. Hold on tight.

The structure of an information process is identical to that of any other process. Structure is about the only thing which is common. The aim, the inputs, and the process itself are substantially different.

The following is a simple view:

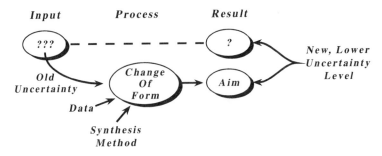

Notice above that three uncertainties entered the process and were reduced to one. Two-thirds of uncertainty was resolved. The aim of information based systems is **uncertainty reduction**. Measurement of THE immediate actual information event process innards is not always practical or possible. Measurement must take a different form. The fact that information happens is exhibited in the measurement of results. Whether it be individuals, groups, business enterprises, or nations, the <u>measurement</u> of the <u>effectiveness</u> is in the <u>results</u>. This is true of all processes but **critical** to information measurement.

There are a number of ways to measure uncertainty reduction. One is testing before and after information receipt - A, B, C, D, F. Another measure is in the test of life or of business life. This is most like the baseball batter. Some people and enterprises have a better batting average. Life is a sufficient test of information entropy . . . if one knows how to measure it. (Refer to Appendix A.)

As it turns out, uncertainty is tightly linked to variability in the output results of all processes. Some groups win consistently, reliably. These are the winners.

The choices made are simply better!! Consistency of positive outcomes is a characteristic of best information practices, best **choices,** and relatively better information content. The measurement takes the form of the differences before and after.

Nonmanufacturing Examples

It is at this point that we often field comments saying "Please give us some nonmanufacturing examples." We already have. Previously (page 11) were listed 20 nonmanufacturing, primarily information services appropriate to all industries.

A few pages earlier the "1 + 1 = 2" example is purely an information process. Before the instructional "news" was given to you or anyone else 1 + 1 = anything. One just didn't know! Given answers at all, the answers will be various. The information received somehow reduced the **outcome choices**. The information content after sufficient instruction changed the choices from "anything" to a consistent, invariable "2". What has happened resulted in increased chances of making better choices.

Consulting is a similar example (in any industry). What consultants deliver to a client company increases the **chances** of **better choices**. More choices go into the information process and fewer, better choices come out.

Diagnostic physicians are mentioned. Consider the case where a five year old child (real case, California, 1967)[10] complains of a back pain. The parents have a lot of choices including doing nothing, "take an aspirin," tough it out, etc. The parents also have a large uncertainty. They lack information. A physician visit is scheduled. Preliminary x-rays indicate that two vertebra had collapsed. For a week the doctor searches for a cause. During this time subsequent x-rays determine a third vertebra collapsed and a fourth deteriorating. There are serious chances for spinal cord damage that could cause paralysis or even death. A second doctor is assigned. The cause remains uncertain.

---

[10]   Ginsberg, A.S., F. L. Offensend. "An Application of Decision Theory to a Medical-Diagnosis Treatment Problem" IEEE Transactions, Vol. SSC-4, No. 3, September 1968, pp. 355-362.

The two physicians organized the information analysis into action choices and outcome possibilities.

This is termed a state matrix. It is shown below:

	Outcomes		
	Cure	*Paralysis*	*Death*
Wait			
Treat			

Actions

Consider that cure means complete cure, and that paralysis means from the neck down (within six months) and that death means probable (within six months).

In order to complete the choices a positive or negative "value" must be attributed to each cell in the matrix. Everyone agreed to the best goal . . . cure.

Now comes a problem. The doctors have a difference of opinion. They do not and can not agree even on the ranking of which is worse; paralysis or death. One considered death to be worse than paralysis. The other considered the reverse. These are value system differences. Their attitudes differ causing them to individually consider different weights on the possible outcomes of the choices.

An important point comes to the surface. Choices may be governed as much by what we want to avoid as what we want to achieve.

The parents now have a choice. Which physician is appropriate?

How Much of a Process is Information?

These are the types of information processes and information content we are considering here. $1+1 = 2$. The parents have two choices. How much is it worth to the parents to make the right choice?

Utility Functions

To satisfy our measurement objective we must merge and quantify two otherwise vague subjects — information and value.[11] Value and utility are the subjects here.

Various disciplines, including psychology, marketing, economics and operations research, encounter the concept of value and seek to explain it. They do so from different perspectives using different vocabularies.

Psychology speaks in terms of:

- Levels of abstraction
- Intrinsic and extensive factors
- Perceptions of benefits and sacrifice.

Clearly, emotional and perceptual attributes have been shown to influence the value placed on objects by people.

Marketing speaks in terms of price and price attributes.

- Value in low price
- Value in whatever I want in a product
- Value is the quality I get for the price I pay
- Value is what I get for what I give.

Price is a numeric indicator that improves our capacity to quantify.

---

[11] For a merging of the two topics into "valuable information," refer to pp. 81-85 and Appendix A: Calculating Information Value, p. 186, and Value and Valuation, p. 188.

Economics speaks in terms of utility preference functions, demand curves, elasticity and diminishing returns. While the previous two disciplines do not attempt to quantify (or measure) the degree of "value," economics does.

Operations Research speaks in terms of objective functions and maximization of goals and **goal gains**.

Here we will use the most quantifiable:

Functional Utility + Emotional Utility

Goal gain in utility is the high value objective.

In order to measure information content (or anything else), we must be able to distinguish (1) the **order of merit** and (2) the **degree of merit**.

We state here that information content is valuable if, and only if, the content contributes to a goal gain in an objective. The objective may be function, emotion or both.

All of the process part of process is information. It is difficult to separate the information about a process from the information in a process from the measurement system of a process.

In an article tracing the 500 year history of the Beretta firearms company, Ramchandran Jaikumar discusses the degree of toughness in this dilemma regarding process reengineering. Beretta said, "The hardest thing mentally in our 500 year history was the shift to understanding the information content in processes."[12]

A good way to begin thinking about the information content in a specific process is to simply take the whole process and subtract out the physical non-informational objects. What remains is the informational **CHOICE** component; some call it the intellectual component. The type of thing we are needing to measure is the process bias.

Information **biases actions** and outcomes. We are searching for measures of bias. Most investigators want to eliminate bias. Here we want to focus on bias. Bias shapes our choices.

We will begin with a simple case of three colored balls. The balls are informational related in their shape. The color of each is very information related. Without color, the balls would all be the same. There would be no difference. Round balls are biased round else they would be cubes or triangles. Color adds another individual bias to distinguish differences.

[12]   Ramchandran Jaikumar, "From Filing and Fitting to Flexible Manufacturing: A Study in the Evolution of Process Control," Harvard Business School Working paper, pp. 88-045, Harvard University Press, 1988.

Obstacles – Too Many Possibilities – Impossible

Often, the encounters with information measures and information optimization as THE ONLY basis for enterprise optimization are incredibly tough, confusing, and frustrating. It is
comforting to remember that most every other meaningful
activity started with the same feeling. Many of life's endeavors
such as: golf, tennis, bridge, business, engineering, race car
driving, teamwork and opposite sex encounters are often as
confusing and frustrating. All this means is that there is missing or invalid information. Certainly it means lacking valuable
information. Recall the topic of "ignorant" people earlier. This
relates to the authors and perhaps the reader!

An information entropy approach is difficult only because we
were not taught it early enough so that we could improve the
approaches through practice. The following are some of the
frequent objections which can be anticipated during the ac-
quaintance with the approach.

Deterministic vs. Probabilistic

People desire guarantees — certainty. Complete and positive
control requires 100 percent certainty. This is ruled out by
nature. There is no perfect information. There are no guarantees with social systems such as business. Path choices and
odds improvement are the best practice. Fortunately, being top
tier does not carry the obligation to be perfect.

First place, winning and leading are achievable by very small
percentage differences relative to the others in the race. We
hope to show exactly where the guarantees exist and where
they do not. It is the closeness or farness from guarantees that
is the measure we seek to define.

Intuitive Entropy

Laws of nature are not required to make sense to us. Rather, we are obliged to make sense of and appreciate the laws. News happens!

In some cases information and information entropy are intuitive and in many cases, not. To the extent of the authors' abilities and with understood imprecision of words rather than mathematical formula, we first will present an intuitive description with words (mostly) and pictures. After the verbal description we will follow with numbers.

— Choices and Chances —

If one is attempting to choose the single "best" object from a set of possibilities (for example the three (3) balls mentioned earlier), then when the task is done one will have been chosen and two will remain. The outcome result of this process is one choice, and the input at the start is, say, one chance to be right and two chances not to be right. Notice that the only barrier to perfection in the choice is uncertainty (lack of information). Luck can happen. This is subsequently addressed.

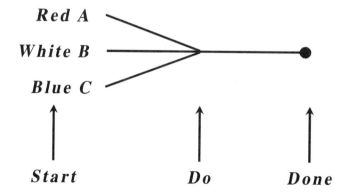

All things being equal and with no other information, the choices are blind and equally likely. **Equal choices** of this sort is the **worst possible** scenario. The arithmetic analyzing this is division.

If we form the division of the output (one choice) divided by the (three) inputs then we can more clearly see what is going to happen. How much information do we have and how much do we need?

$$\frac{(\,1\,) = One\ output\ choice\ result}{(\,3\,) = One\ right\ choice + two\ not\ right\ choices} = 1/3$$

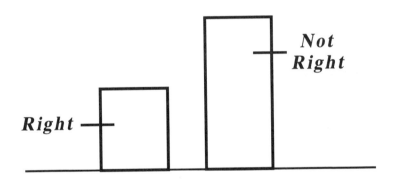

Probability theory argues that one possesses one-third of the information necessary to make perfect choices. Energy laws say that energy must be expended to improve the outcome. What we need is better information.

To improve the outcome, information must be gained **ahead of time** to better identify the correct choice or reduce the "not right" choices. The information needs to exactly **match** the situation to be pertinent. The context and content must be on target. This might be easy.

The library might have the answer and one could go research it. For example, one might find in the literature "the red ball is never the right ball in red, white, blue set." Or one could forecast that it may take two trials to find the correct ball and go ahead and pick the red ball to see what happens. What will happen is a consequence that will yield information for "next" time.

"Behind time" can be converted to "ahead of time" if the activity is to be repeated. Notice in either case there is an expenditure of energy to reduce the uncertainty. The gain in certainty comes at the expense of energy expenditure.

If one happens to "know" (from library research or from previous trial) that the red ball is **not a right choice** then the situation changes. All balls may still be present but the red ball is virtually **ruled out**. Been there, done that!

Thus the resulting arithmetic is:

$$\frac{(\,1\,) = One\ output\ choice\ result}{(\,2\,) = One\ perfect\ choice + one\ incorrect\ + one\ known\ wrong} = \mathbf{\mathit{1/2}}$$
$$\qquad\qquad\quad (\,1\,) \qquad\qquad (\,1\,) \qquad\qquad (\,0\,)$$

In effect the information helped alter the situation to:

$$\frac{1\ Choice}{2\ Choice}\quad Or\ 1/2\ Versus\ 1/3\ Previously$$

The difference in profiles before and after the information change is shown below.

1/3 Before   1/2 After

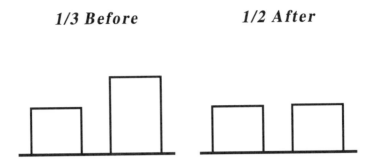

The "information" about the red ball biased the choices so that it was eliminated as a choice.

Now we have perhaps confused ourselves. Previously it was stated that the "uniform" distribution was the worst possible discrete distribution. That is what we achieved here. The one half graph "looks" more uniform. The information content is apparently higher and the uncertainty level lower. What is happening?

Confusion often happens in separating information inside a process, information about a process and measurement information of a process consequence. Nowhere is this apt to be more severe than when the process is a probability process (reliability for example).

In the case at hand three unfortunate choices may have led to confusion in the outcome. First, the discussion took the viewpoint from inside the process and describes what is happening **during the doing.** Second, we never got to the "done" point, therefore, we did not achieve the goal of measuring results.

Third, there are rules that achieve proper measurement which were violated. Measurement of a process must include the before "start" and after "done." Measuring the middle does not constitute a full measure.

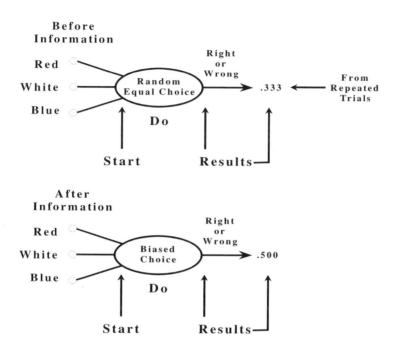

The distribution of the top case is the worst case where the outcome matches a uniform distribution and there is a greater number of choices. With no learning (forgetfulness) the odds and chances remain one in three. The second case outcome is biased to a "better uniform" and thus infers that information somehow entered the choice process. Chances of one in two are "better" than one in three.

Notice in the before/after histogram how easy it was to forget that we ruled out one choice. Both cases started with three balls.

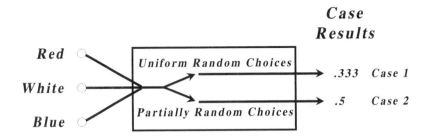

Since we know (it was proven) that information is the only way to control outcomes, we know that differing outcomes absolutely represent different information content.

A good way to think of this case is the "difference between guessing and knowing."

Those interested in monetizing might consider that the "correct" ball contained a financial reward inside. The economic payoff occurs after the outcome of the choice. The "expected" value of knowing about the red ball is calculable.

Events where choices and chances are a part include business, bridge, golf and life. Certain people or groups consistently operate at a success rate well above the natur1l odds. The extent to which this happens is a measure c i their information content.

Information Entropy and Processes During Construction

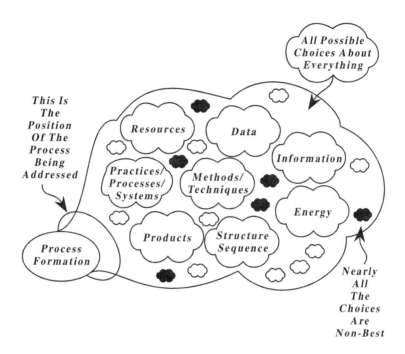

Consider the creation of an economic engine process and the elements associated. As any process is formed (or reformed) choices must be made as to what, which and how much of each ingredient to include.

Choices also must be made as to the structure, order, sequence and redundancy of synthesizing or integrating the process input objects toward final conclusion. There is no avoiding these choices.

Choices must be made if the process is made whole. Not choosing is a choice. The very act of including one choice also excludes the alternative possibilities. The process is certainly biased by the inclusions and exclusions.

For each choice and each collection of choices there are possibilities. Often there are many possible choices. Each class of choice may carry with it bad, good and perhaps best possibilities. Normally, there are **more bad choice possibilities** and fewer good or best. Best is exclusive. [13]

Thus, to **blindly pick holds the high odds of a non-best choice.** The previous sentence is going to be terribly important later. Knowingly or not, the choices are made.

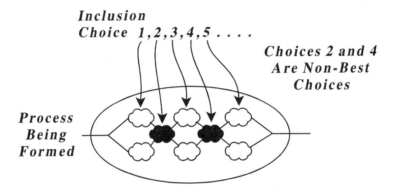

The thing that changes the odds in the choices is information. Given incentive to create best results, the only reason for not choosing the best items is uncertainty or false certainty.

Uncertainty is missing information . . . so is false certainty. The **process is then the sum of the choices** each being uncertain to some degree. Thus, the total amount of lack of information is measured by the resulting **imperfection** and the total amount of information is measured by the amount of results **goodness.**

---

13   Best may not be singular. Later we will illustrate the archer and the arrow. Several trajectories can hit the target.

The characteristic which gauges or measures the goodness of choices and ingredients is contribution to variance in the intended outcome. If the outcomes are consistently on target, then the choices have been good (information). The figure below illustrates a case where the outcome is the same as the aim.

Exact Content & Content Match

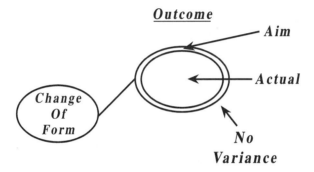

If the choices are good and best, then there will be minimal variance in the actual result to the aim. To the extent that bad choices are chosen or creep in unknowingly then variance will appear in the outcome.

Some of the choices contribute to variance either individually or in combination.

Although difficult, hold the constant thought that some variances are positive such that actual results exceed the aim.[14] These positive contributors to variance need to be cherished.

---

[14]   For the similar input, exceptional results occur.

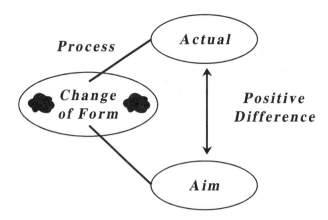

The resulting difference between actual and aim is a consequence of the choices that have become part of the process. In
the case where actual exceeds aim, an inquiry may be appropriate into the aiming process as well as the ingredients chosen.

Entropy Emergence

The resulting process which has been formed is DIFFERENT
on the inside than on the outside. The process bubble has been
formed to include fewer and, perhaps, better inputs, process
sequence, energy application than random selection would
yield. The restricted space inside the process causes an entropy
difference.

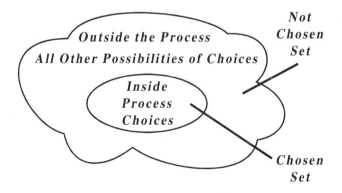

The restricted ingredients and their order inside the process are no longer the same as the outside. It is an anomaly. It is different. It is more orderly — guaranteed. The process is biased. Whether the process is good different or bad different is yet to be determined. The very process of choosing is a large part of the information entropy.

The information is transported to the process and is an imprint on the conduct. Information is **transportable**.

In the best process or practice, all of the choices will need to be informed selections. This would have required extremely good information. Since the choices were all informational and the process activity conduct is all informational, one could say that the information entropy of a process is a result of all choices made constructing the actual result. One may consider that the degree of information inherent in the choosing has flowed into the process accompanying the structure.

Note: We have found that the very name "thermodynamics" frightens some away and disassociates others from the remotest possibility that there could be a linkage. Consider that the name of the topic was given long ago by folks creating steam engines. Consider that were it named today it might well have an information name. There is an organizational element in the rule which is most interesting. It is not the energy typically taught.

Freedom, Choices and Restrictions

Any and every process necessarily restricts freedoms. A difference is generated outside versus inside the process. Choices are different inside versus outside. This is the difference.[15] Processes bind sequence, context, method, intensity, rate and operation application constraining outcomes.

The restrictions channel (direct, encourage, order, control) the collective activity or energy devotion and other intermediate resultants toward the process outcome aim. The name "**control**" is commonly associated with this construct.

The Second Law of Energy does not favor extremes in either order or disorder but it does permit each temporarily. The ebb and flow of differences is huge.

Information inherently controls the transformation of incoming ingredients through various state and form changes to accomplish an outcome form. The notion of eliminating choices destructive to aim and encouraging aim enhancing choices is the element of **control**. The information **biases possibilities**. This notion is important in process construction and measurement. Consider that process is the transformation coordination of inputs toward outcomes. Remember, the output of information processes and the information component of all processes is greater certainty or less uncertainty.

More restrictive (tighter control) processes stringently reduce or limit the choices or variety of structural paths available. At the upper limit the process is so precisely rigid that only one path exists and the outcome is certain. There is no choice. The result is deterministic — one and only one outcome. High **control** is in evidence.

---

[15] Ludwig Boltzmann's quantification of energy entropy is extensible to this case. $S = k \log W$. "S" (entropy) is less inside the process because "W" (the number of available choices) is smaller (restricted). In this formulation, a minus sign (-) is always inferred but only sometimes explicit in the writing because "k" can represent the negative aspect. We are explicit in computational formulations but not in the conversation text.

Less restrictive (looser) processes provide larger variety or numbers of choices and thus more paths. Tighter control requires higher information content so that each process bound element is constantly more exactly certain of efficient energy deployment toward accomplishing the process outcome aim. The energy cost to achieve results is less when the process or practice "knows."

There is still no implication of goodness at this point concerning freedom, control or variance. It is rather like the difference in pattern of a shotgun and rifle. Both tight and loose process **control** have application.

Aim Information vs. Production Information

If the goal, purpose or aim of the process is fixed (static), then any variance in the outcome must be attributed to process and especially also to lack of (process internal) information. Similarly, successes are attributable to proper processes and proper information especially. If the target is moving (dynamic), information concerning the target position must be properly projected and communicated to the process control points to dynamically alter the ingredients.

If the design of the aiming mechanism is flawed, a perfectly good process will be aimed at a false target (and "miss"). The resulting variance in the outcome is caused in this instance by the informational guidance system. Successful outcomes in dynamic situations are a consequence of the proper collaboration of the process and aiming information. The design of feedback events is different in dynamic systems (shorter time increments, for example).

The Statistical Connection

Statements, measures and analysis methods follow statistical forms when information is defined as the degree of certainty (or uncertainty) about an event, state, object or topic. Economic or financial quantification must be applied independently following the statistical form. Actualization moves from future possibilities to current realities to past history.

Given that a process is purpose aimed and that achievement of purpose can be measured, then it follows that the goodness or precision of the process is linked to the degree of achieving the purpose aimed. Measurement of the "hits" (successes) and "misses" (failure) would constitute a measure of the degree of **outcome control** and also of the information or lack of it.

The degree of **outcome control** of the process thus is linked to the degree of certainty in producing an exactly targeted outcome. If the process is certain (perfect information), each outcome will be on target (invariant). To the degree that uncertainty (choice, freedom) exists, variance is a distinct possibility. Thus, observations and measures of goal variance also speak to information deficiencies. **Process variation and goal variation are measurable forms of information content presence.**

The vocabulary becomes statistical because of the requirement to know information ahead of time and to express the part one knows from the part one doesn't know.

The Energy Connection

All forms of energy are subject to the same laws. Transformation processes adhere to the natural laws of energy (a law called The Second Law). The particular aspect we are seeking is not the energy per se but the **orderliness** component of energy. All people, including those conducting business, are bound to adhere to natural law processes.

This is the real law of how "news" works! Energy devoted earlier in study and practice causes information to be transformed and stored as intellect. This happens with individuals, **groups** and **enterprises**. The release of the stored knowledge (previously paid for information) is the energy application selecting ingredient choices during formation or conduct of processes (and during the doing).

The resulting order, sequence, intensity of energy investment or consumption in a process provokes orderly outcomes to a variable degree. To the degree that equal outcomes require less process energy, the choices have been better. More for less is better! One energy (information) creates leverages in other forms of energy. Variance in the aimed outcome is connected to the energy and also is measurable. Entropy is commonly used as the energy flow rate. Not only is it flow rate but the **organization,** order and coherence of the flow rate. The pressure differential (inside versus outside the process) resulting from illuminations of paths and pursuit of paths cause behaviors inside to be different from behaviors outside. Variation and entropy are connected. Higher choice, looser systems possess higher entropy and exhibit greater variation (higher confusion and greater "shuffledness"). Lower choice, more orderly systems possess lower entropy and less variations.

The People Connection

Information exchange and synthesis are powerful capabilities that people possess over other objects in Nature. The capacity to remember and to record history is powerful. The ability to conduct and direct collaborative activity is conditional on accurate, reliable, timely and meaningful information. Information compels a change in action direction.

Given that the process topic is business, people (sometimes machine supported) are participating in the various rules of construction, coordination and consumption. The human energies, both physical and mental, are integral to business process. Except in the machine to machine closed system, people are the **action directors**. Even in the all machine case, people are only a step removed, having both manufactured the machines and chosen them. If the people are not aimed at all (aimless) or are not properly aimed, then variance is likely despite the apparently precise machinery.

People perform roles in the information, decision, energy, devotion and control aspects. Communication coordinates and binds the participating process elements. Although hazardous to do so, people often are used exclusively as the measuring instruments for process control. Recall earlier when people could not see the triangles or the light blinking. Decision forks are people oriented (choices). Action is a people choice. Directed action is guaranteed to be information biased.

Programmable Devices

The question arises as to whether computerized information is better or different than humanized information. Given that variance is a measure of information goodness, it seems to follow that computers possess better information because properly programmed computing devices operate invariably.

Both the definition of information (anything that makes difference) and its measure (variation) remain steadfast through the man-machine scenario.

In the context of computers, people are computers too! The human mind is constructed like a largely parallel electrochemical computer. The mind is able to simultaneously and continuously synthesize great amounts of new data input joining it with previous data to arrive at courses of action. Most often the mind ends up with multiple approximate answers as opposed to one. All parallel processing does this.

Recall the earlier student workgroups. Action choices are then a matter of selecting the appropriate response for the situation. A small amount of information makes the difference in response choices, particularly nearly equal choices.

Silicon (and other firmware) computers, as we know them now, are more precise (given the "proper" instructions) in executing the tasks for which they can be reliably programmed. Both the construction and programming of computers is an energy consumption transformation activity that follows The Second Law.

What is happening is that the transferal exactly conforms to Second Law transformations. Humans are constructing information tools to reduce variances that are important to them. Knowledge is transformed. People literally instruct the machines with information transactions (called rules). This practice is common. Recall earlier the rules programming of church, government, etc.

The net result is that valuable information is valuable regardless of the source. Valuable information can come from anywhere . . . and usually does.

Exactly What Are We Measuring?

What is the probability that a natural process transforms inputs to a greater output magnitude or power than the inputs?

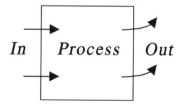

Whatever the measure, in whatever units (or convertible units), the sum of the outputs will necessarily exceed the sum of the inputs.

$$\Sigma \; Outs > \Sigma \; Ins$$

In this relationship *"Out"* is accelerated over *"In."* We often call this performance. We need more *out* for less *in* to achieve performance.

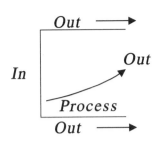

Regardless of the exact formula or reason or whatever, the graph of "out" greater than "in" is the region of performance of the shaded region.

The line where output is equal to input is the separation line.

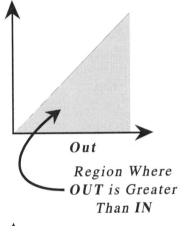

Out

Region Where
OUT is Greater
Than IN

Unfortunately there is a little problem here with the natural laws — perpetual motion. If the outputs are greater than the inputs then we will have created perpetual motion. The patent office forbids issuing a patent for perpetual motion.

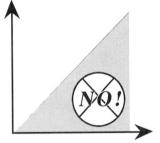

Therefore, the answer to the original question is zero. The probability is zero that a natural process transforms the output to a greater energy state than the input state.

$$Pr \{ \Sigma\, Outs > \Sigma\, Ins \} = 0.0$$

How Revolting!

This is bad news! This cannot be right! But it is. Both performance and profit happen. Profit happens!

> *That Is Why We Call It Work Instead Of Fun!*

What we call profit is a term that was invented to describe the socialization of the natural laws of (energy) exchange and trading. Although it is forbidden to manufacture new energy directly, it is permitted to exchange energy between and among groups and processes. Profit arises from exchanging and borrowing from others. Eventually this all must add up to be exactly on the line shown earlier where output is equal to input. Another law of the same energy set says exactly that.

What the natural energy laws say about processes may be recalled from physics.

- Something for nothing does not exist naturally.
- Everything balances moment by moment in energy terms or it is in the act of doing so eventually.
- Exchange between processes is permitted. Up trades and down trades are okay so long as the energy bank balances.
- Energy transfers are directional in nature.
- Absolute perfect energy is forbidden and so is perfect information. Isn't this a remarkable coincidence!

The above bullets represent the part typically instructed. It is the deterministic "always completely happens" part.

The part which applies to communication, chances, choices, processes, systems, time, information and organization follows.

What exactly we are measuring is the amount or degree of **organizational content** that is known goal directed as separated from the content which is not.

The feature of energy of which we are most critically interested is the subtle (secret) organizational aspect. When Humpty Dumpty fell off the wall what happened? He gathered kinetic energy on the way to the ground **exactly equal** to that required to put him back. However, when he hit the ground Humpty shattered and part of the collision dissipated in heat. To put Humpty Dumpty back together one would need to scrape up and recover all the energy pieces. More than that the energy would need to be **sorted back into order**. The two things come in pairs, energy and its organization. Both need to be restored for Humpty Dumpty. It is this organizational aspect of energy upon which we derive the informational property.

The natural laws very much favor exchanges to be neutral, zero difference transactions. Eventually all the swapping and bartering of energy must zero balance. This is rather like transfer pricing "at cost." The equilibrium tendency is for exchanges to be "tit-for-tat" equal. There is minimum differential. These are uniform transactions.

Relative to information, nature encourages that half (half yes, half no) the information on a situation be known. Nature's saying might be: "Give everyone a 50-50 chance." Nature likes averages rather than extremes.

As much as any other thing here is the distinction between single objects and groups of objects. Much instruction is devoted to single actions and reactions. The treatment here is much more interested in organization focusing and behavior of **groups of objects**. Differences don't exist until multiple objects enter the picture. Likewise, averages and variations **only** exist among multiples.

There is a tax required on any and all changes in type and/or form. Nature frowns on perfect anything. Form changes are guaranteed to be taxed with an efficiency tax. Sorting of a list is a form change. Constructing a sentence is a form change. These change the organization content. There will be imperfections in the exchanges. We often call this exhaust, waste, residue, error or inefficiency.

Think of the platform diver entering the water with minimum splash — no waves. If the dive is really perfect there will be no waves, not even a ripple. The waves are information evidence of the character (greatness) of the dive. The average diver will make bigger waves relative to the perfect dive.

We say here and measure that the evidence in the result is conditioned by the control and information content of the diver. The waves, made up of water, got disorganized by the diver.

Do not be too quick to judge the energy waste as bad. For example, the waste waves given off from the imperfections of the nuclear furnace exchanges of our sun are the same waves that give us light, heat, fuel, and life itself. In essence, we live from the exhaust residue of the imperfect sun. Perhaps we should rethink pollution . . . just kidding.

It might be clearer now why it is easier to measure waste than perfection. Perfection causes less waves and tends toward invisible. The waves of imperfection are more frequent and visible. In perfection, there are simply no differences; no waves, nothing happening during perfectly equal swaps. Consider carefully the case where all students receive 100.

To the observer, perfection may take the form of voids, vacuums, absences, invisibilities, nothings and black holes. Nature is auditable in this regard also. The absence of waves is information too. Sometimes the news is in the silence, and sometimes the news is imbedded in the noise.

When the law says nothing is perfect, it means it. Nothing is perfect. This is good! The waves of natural imperfections give us life. In one context they are energy, in another context the waves are information. This is tough!

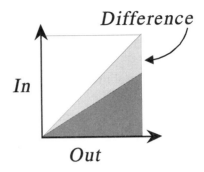

The operative word in the previous discussion is "natural." All by itself nature does not and cannot create order. We can. By applying or borrowing exceptional energy, the normal trend of nature can be "pushed" in the "unnatural" more orderly direction.

The input-process-output graph then takes the customary form. The "profit" of the process is then the positive difference which is created beyond natural equilibrium. The information which we shall measure is the amount necessary to construct an organized exchange differential among the various partner processes willing to borrow or exchange energy. In order to measure this differential, the process in question simply **must** make different **choices** from natural.

Applications

People often inquire as to where and which situations are appropriate for being "solved" by this technique. This is akin to asking where energy applies or alternately where information applies.

This is a natural law of science. It works full time everywhere on all things on this earth and most likely the universe. There is **no immunity**.

It applies to and is used to explain order and disorder in hot and cold, energy, communications, language, music and other media forms, business systems, group systems, social systems, governmental systems, learning systems, process engineering and reengineering, accounting, much of psychology, much of sociology, chemistry, physics, electricity, and computers. More importantly, **all** business **success** can be explained in terms of this law as well as **all** business **failures**.

Uncertainty in where, when and how to order, focus and direct resource investment is success critical.

The evidence of exceptional outcome control is the evidence of valuable privileged information. Whether the goal is golf, bridge, business or horse races, the exemplars possess particular information that is far beyond luck.

Valuable Information Economic Value

The economic value of information is calculated as the proportional amount of goal controlling information content times the total economic goal consequence PLUS the proportional goal unaligned information content times the natural equilibrium economic goal consequence.

Restated this means that the expected information worth is an amount equal to the fractional degree of certainty times the size of the reward plus the degree of uncertainty times the natural equilibrium result.

At one end of the scale is certainty and the rewards from deterministic knowledge. At the other end is blind ignorance and luck arising from no knowledge whatever.

5. DIFFERENCES

USEFUL AND NECESSARY INFORMATION (VERSUS) VALUABLE INFORMATION

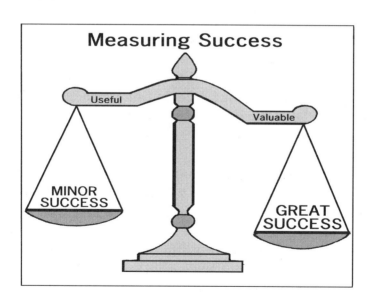

Judgment vs. Measurement of Worth

A strong axiom in value determination is the inappropriateness of determining self worth. Although self-esteem is good, value is attributed to an object by outsiders. In information processes the value is primarily attributed by the receiver. In business context this is the customer.

The sender may possess judgment (good or bad) concerning value, but the measurement must be accomplished by and/or communicated directly or indirectly back by the receiver. Participants inside an enterprise are both biased and unknowing about specific customer valuation criteria unless feedback information is forthcoming from the correct "source."

Information behaves the same. There must be a **context and content match** between what the sender sends and the receiver needs.

In social and business terms, the value is settled during the exchange process. Things (including information) are **worth more** than the exchange fee to **each** and **both** sides. Price or fee exchange is at the center of each different exchange.

Accounting has little hope of implementing value accounting. Valuing firm objects is beyond the accounting scope let alone information objects. Kenneth Boulding explains it this way: "the economist . . . looks on the accountant as a man who has to perform an impossible task. He has first to reduce what is essentially a multidimensional reality to a one-dimensional figure; and in the second place, he has to do this on the basis of knowledge about the future which he cannot possibly have."[16]

---

[16]   K.E. Boulding, "Economics and Accounting: The Uncongenial Twins," in Studies in Accounting Theory, W.T. Baster and Sidney Davidson, Irwin Inc. 1962, p. 53.

Howard Snavely addresses the same issue: "The degree of probability needed before phenomena may be accepted as evidence has **not been established**."

Again Snavely. "It should be reasonably evident by now that the evaluation of a managerial policy or past act or decision is even more difficult than either the valuation of a firm or the evaluation of management as a whole."

"A little reflection will show that it is <u>impossible</u> to separate and to report the results of each past decision, for to do so requires going back to the original decision and tracing results of all possibilities (branches of the decision tree) that were taken as well as all alternatives that were not taken."[17]

Rather than being impossible as suggested here, the measurement must be implemented DIFFERENTLY. Value and worth are measured as shown in the appendices and in the remainder of this text.

It is the inability to deal with and accept uncertainty that is the severe barrier. Reliability engineering cannot exist to the accountant . . . but it does. Value engineering cannot exist to the accountant . . . but it does. Profit engineering cannot exist to the accountants . . . because they believe they are it . . . but they are not. It is not impossible at all. Impossible in this case is only a matter of lack of information.

---

[17]   Snavely, Howard J., "Accounting Information Criteria," <u>The Accounting Review</u>, April, 1967.

Reductionism vs. Holism; Separation vs. Integration

Reductionists tend to be contemptuous of holists, for they feel they alone have the key to the universe. Holists know they have a broad perspective, a large insight, whereby they can see all the riches missed by the single-minded reductionist. In principle it would appear so easy to be both at once, but human nature is evidently such that it enjoys taking positions on philosophical or political doctrines.

Our approach here leaves room for both since by observation of nature both have existed and will continue to do so.

A key to the pragmatic approach is held in Operations Research studies. Optimization of the separate components does not guarantee optimization of the whole. Score one point for the holists. The whole is greater than the sum of the parts. But optimization requires precise action by each and every part; without fail. Score one for the reductionists.

Value definitely aggregates upward and thresholds of detection may only surface at various points. If value exists at all, it usually is only visible at the whole. For conservation of energy purposes in measurement, it seems prudent to first measure the whole before separating the parts.

In the information process structure view, one could suspect that the holists are considering the aiming and guidance portion of the process, and the reductionists are performing actions in support of the aim (production). Both possess critical information requiring connection, one to the other. Perhaps one must consider the possibility that teamwork is required.

Useful Information Characteristics

The Information Advantage contains sections on rules. The purpose of rules is to rule some things in and other things out. (Recall the previous section on process choices.)

Accounting has implemented rules on the definition of "useful" information. Recall the list:[18]

$$\left.\begin{array}{l} \textit{Relevant} \\ \textit{Reliable} \\ \textit{Understandable} \\ \textit{Significant} \\ \textit{Practical} \\ \textit{Sufficient} \end{array}\right\} = \textit{Useful Information}$$

Accounting also ruled "in" CERTAINTY by requiring tangible, reliable evidence, records, documents. The profession "ruled" that it could **not deal with uncertainty**.

These rules guarantee that the accounting profession is trapped in the past. More than this, by ruling in "useful," the accounting theory ruled out "valuable." Accounting rules destined the resulting information to be **useful old regular non-valuable** information.

Worse still the accounting profession ruled itself "right" and ignored even working on valuable. Worse than that the profession claimed the territory complete and refused resources and/or admonished those pursuing the "impossible" extensions. *Shame.*

---

[18]   The Information Advantage, op.cit., pp. 148, 404, 452-459.

The future is quite easily determined to the extent that business requires. Stochastic (probabilistic) dynamic games are a case in point. The masters certainly win in bridge, poker, gin and so on. This is not luck. It is valuable information. Casinos are much more in control of profitability than most enterprises.[19]

As an indication of the size of the void which exists in the topic, the criteria for valuable information does not exist elsewhere that we could find. The criteria for valuable information must literally combine the criteria for valuable **plus** the criteria for information. This requires a sense of value engineering plus information engineering.

One needs to consider the possibility that REALLY current (timely) data is not in the computer because it has not yet been entered and REALLY exclusive information (as in secrets) possibly won't be either. REALLY valuable, REALLY exclusive may get REALLY closely held.[20]

It is a bit misleading and unfair to leave an impression that little work has been accomplished in the topic. The contrary is true, particularly in the military. The "G2" intelligence community speaks of, and implements, Essential Elements of Information (EEIs) needed in battlefield situations. Commanders critical information requirements (CCIRs) are instructed, as are "red teams" for alternative assessments.

Our comments here apply to the larger commercial sector and/ or to the totality of information. Most particularly, what we were seeking were the criteria upon which to differentiate valuable from good from useful and so on. The criteria are difficult to find.

---

[19]   The Information Advantage, op. cit., pp. 471-478. To view exactly how this control happens review the Blackjack example.

[20]   For a review of the subject of value see Utility Functions p. 49. Also refer to Appendix A: Calculating Information Value p. 186 and Value and Valuation p. 188 for discussions of information value.

The combined criteria are offered in the following diagram.[21]

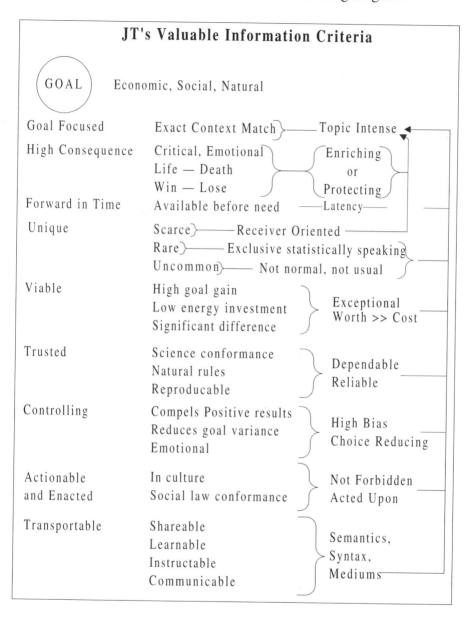

JT's Valuable Information Criteria

GOAL   Economic, Social, Natural

Goal Focused	Exact Context Match	— Topic Intense
High Consequence	Critical, Emotional / Life — Death / Win — Lose	Enriching or Protecting
Forward in Time	Available before need	—Latency—
Unique	Scarce — Receiver Oriented / Rare — Exclusive statistically speaking / Uncommon — Not normal, not usual	
Viable	High goal gain / Low energy investment / Significant difference	Exceptional Worth >> Cost
Trusted	Science conformance / Natural rules / Reproducable	Dependable Reliable
Controlling	Compels Positive results / Reduces goal variance / Emotional	High Bias Choice Reducing
Actionable and Enacted	In culture / Social law conformance	Not Forbidden Acted Upon
Transportable	Shareable / Learnable / Instructable / Communicable	Semantics, Syntax, Mediums

---

[21]   A more complete discussion of the criteria is presented in <u>Ahead of Time</u>, op. cit.

> **Valuable Information exactly relates to high conse-
> quence actions and arrives ahead of time so that goal
> gain controlling action can be taken with relatively
> unique certainty. The odds are improved beyond
> natural.**

"Quantifiable" is a candidate for inclusion. It is omitted on the logic that if and when numbers are valuable information then they fit the criteria given.

The criteria for valuable information attempt to rule "in" the full span of exceptional differential information and rule out the routine, useful and necessary because the criteria for marginal value are different.

The primary criteria are that information be receiver oriented and valued above cost. Although the context here is business oriented, no media form is ruled out (the reason for not requiring quantification) and neither, for example, is humor. Large consequence information does not require that it be serious if, for example, the receiver needs and highly values non-serious.

To be able to confidently act, alter choices, and perhaps capitalize on the fragments of information (tips) received, the content must be trusted. The authenticity must not be in doubt, otherwise the new information which is supposed to reduce doubt creates doubt instead. This opens topics including integrity and reliability of the source. Who are you to believe?

Know Valuable When One Sees It

The eyeball cannot see the eye, the fish cannot see the water. People who think they can detect valuable information are often mistaken. This is where the instrument thing that we harp on arises. The evidence is measurable and detectable. For all practical purposes valuable information is mostly invisible. First, it is rare by definition, therefore, the incidence and occurrences (practice) are less. Second, the characteristics have never been defined until now. Third, it is not instructed. Fourth, there is noise and clutter obscuring and contaminating the message stream. Fifth, recall the self-worth thing, valuable information is reflected from others. This makes it doubly invisible. Sixth, most believe it is impossible to crack and therefore refuse to work on it. (This is actually good. Those that can see overcome those that cannot!)

However, the improbability is what makes the pursuit more challenging, significant, consequential and valuable. Valuable information is happening, can be designed to be provoked, can be detected and can be measured. Information differentials are at the essence. We will briefly touch upon detection and hope that after the measurement that there will be more clarity.

Until recently the subject was held hostage by virtue of not appreciating the high positive consequence. The characteristic of **transportability** was missing and therefore was an art form.

Now, through the high investment and low returns in computers and technology, attention is being focused. In the confusion, clarity may happen. Refer to the chaos section later.

Computers and technology were intended to create controlled order and make things simpler . . . more convenient.

Computers were intended to control choices and implement regimen. A peculiar thing happened along the path. Instead of reducing choice, technology made **more choice** possible. In information terms and by our measurement criteria **more choice** means **more chances for uncertainty which means more information deficiency**.

Think about it. It is literally true. The good news is that we can create and manufacture about anything we want to. The bad news is that we don't have the information to know what to do. Confusion resulted rather than order. Thus, computers have caused anti-information. "A fool with a tool, is still a fool."

History, Time, Ahead of Time and Timeless

Another book has been constructed concerning how to know things before they happen. The name is <u>Ahead of Time</u>.

For purposes here, consider that some things are timeless. One of the convenient things about timeless objects is the virtue of not being time dependent. Thus, timeless objects are ALWAYS ahead of time. Earlier we mentioned that the primary natural laws are indifferent toward time. The Second Law, in particular, and all of the energy laws are time mindful. One knows ahead of time what is most likely to happen! Get it? Review the upcoming reliability example.

The Enterprise Consequence

Having high probability positive outcomes on your side as a best business partner is a strong ally. Information as presented here is **the controlling entity** of enterprise life. Like it or not certain "news" is powerful. Information or lack of it controls, through choices, the actions toward or away from goal achievement.

Information or lack of it governs careers, enterprises, nations. Less familiar forms govern life itself. Information is proven to be the only controlling entity. The value creating capacity of an enterprise is dependent on possessing the information advantage — period.

To the extent that control of positive outcomes toward business aim or purpose is consequential, then all of the energy consumption as well as the change in form of the ingredients and outcomes have a social consequence which will naturally and artificially possess economic consequence. People are forced, by the very nature of survival, to perform some manner of sustaining economic activity.

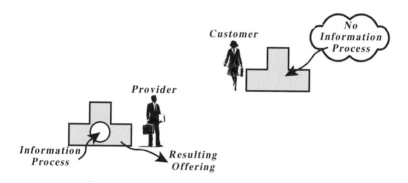

The early Indo-European word for "organization" and "organism" was "worg" from which the modern word for work is derived. A process can sustain work only when its internal energy is purposively organized and directed. This takes information.

If an enterprise has weak information or goal critical omissions then it follows that actualizing desired outcomes in the critical topic will be difficult, costly and time consuming. The symptom will be high variance to goal achievement. Many of the customer choices are not good and the entropy is high.

The enterprise, for very good (but ignorance enhancing) reasons, avoided investing in forming the requisite process, making errors, experiencing variance, reforming processes, trying, failing, fixing and finally "getting right things right." Chances are high that to start from scratch will be tough and expensive. "Things are just not working well!"

This scenario occurs in customer exchange situations. The customer will pay a high price to start from scratch and search the information to satisfy the uncertainty. What customers don't know is the high price they are "paying" daily for information illnesses. The manifestation in the uninformed enterprise is always lackluster or low return on invested energy. By another name this means low profit. Information illness causes low ROI and low P=R-C. Blind spots and low rigor in look ahead techniques cause much of the harm.

The fundamental principle of Return on Investment requires continuous choices among a list of always changing alternative items upon which to invest energy which will return the greatest future value for the energy invested. Although big guidance choices may manifest with the "Financial Allocation Group" the opportunity **cascades** to all task levels.

This process and practice breaks down in two prominent ways. First, if objects of high return are not on the list (incompleteness), then blind spots are present such that best choices are impossible. Best choices may be omitted from consideration. Second, if either the investment or the return or both are not computable or are computed in error (either inflated or deflated) then the list is inappropriately biased (which is what faulty information does). Again, the consequence is non-best choice. Return follows investment. Return is in the future. There is little rigor in calculating the future.

The table below is an example.

Investment Choices

	Investment In	Return Out	Performance Out/In
A	10	12	12/10 = 1.2
B	20	50	50/20 = 2.5
C	6	10	10/6 = 1.7
D	14	14	14/14 = 1.0
E			
F		*What If These Are Missing But Superior To Those Listed?*	
G			

If powerful items such as processes, information, reliability, prevention, energy, customer worth of offerings, time, competency, etc., are not on the list at all or the worth is not calculable, then . . . ??????? stuff happens!! Not good stuff!!

The reliability example (Appendix B) includes both elements. First, reliability is predictive in that it projects <u>future</u> failures and successes of systems and of components. The accounting form of reliability is a much different form of reliability engineering and was presented as the documented past.

The High Value Information Enterprise

"Exemplar" enterprises were mentioned earlier relative to average. The following description is offered to get a feel for the properties of an information rich enterprise.

The value-driven, strong enterprise knows intimately the distinct difference it makes to its customers. This is valuable information. Evidence of this knowledge is strongly reflected in all key communications.

The information wise enterprise implements policies that focus on and bias the economic difference engine. Processes are structured and aimed to create the offerings which, in turn, create substantial positive customer differences. The information processes are defined and connected to the economic engine. Each process is evaluated on the basis of the degree of total worth generating contribution or other equally appropriate value criteria. Key people who contribute to profitability are known and listed by name, regardless of age, current organization, or current title. Information systems are constructed to target valuable information. High worth generating skills and competencies are recruited, trained, and retrained in economic balance. There are few mysteries.

Fresh abilities are developed through information moments provoked by courseware that is valuable information oriented and core competency related. Decision groups evaluate and act on placing investment — encouraging higher potency in customer offerings and capturing an appropriatel / high fair share. All decision groups possess method and techniques that enable them to measure the true worth of enterpri e entities, including products, suppliers, personnel, processes, and systems. Lists exist where the line items are placed in goal achievement order, highest to lowest. As a result of these best practices, analysis of the investment profile of cost is coordinated and explained relative to the customer worth profile. There exists an attitude in the people where it is unthinkable not to be contributing maximum economic engine power.

The people explain their work tasks in terms of the profit contribution that **customers receive**, relative to the share benefit (price) that their activity commands in the customer product or service offering. The result is manifested in high return.

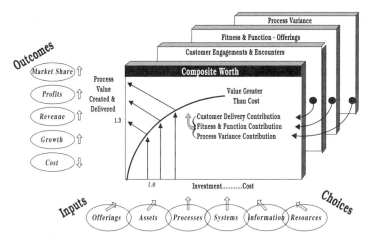

Business behaves in a fashion similar to a big multiple choice quiz. Each enterprise and all its people make **choices of ingredients** to use, processes to construct, market offerings to offer for exchange with others who also have choices of constructing the object themselves or choosing from the objects constructed by others.

The goals of enterprises are among the **outcomes** shown. "Work" is a word we use to describe the exchange process.

6. MEASURE AND SCALE

**The SCALE &
MEASURE OF INFORMATION**

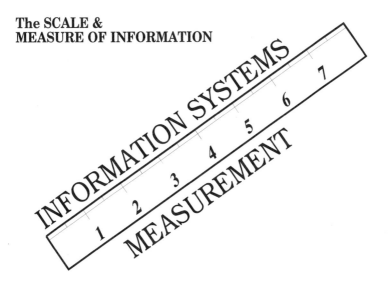

THE NUMBERS

The Measurement Connection

A most important consideration is WHERE in a process the data measurement is viewed, extracted or taken. The bulk or weight of data is not the measure of information. Our measure of information is the difference in action consequence which results!! The output point, or beyond, is of high interest.

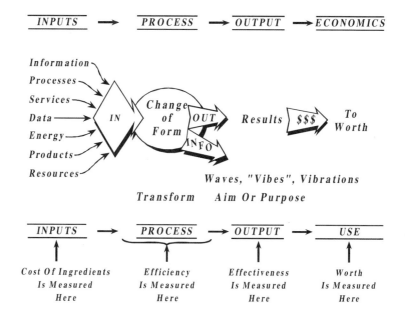

Note that the waves, "vibes," vibrations arrow in the diagram addresses the imperfections, such as waste or scrap, that occur in every process and that reduce the efficiency of converting inputs to outputs. Information processes create variances, vibrations and noise.

The next sections are intended to further clarify these issues. As shown in the diagram efficiency, effectiveness and worth are measured at **different positional points**. This is **huge**.

Efficiency is a consumption measure at and during the form change regarding the energy and ingredients (including waste and scrap) consumed in the construction of the results. Effectiveness is measured at the point of results regarding the meeting or not meeting of output standards.

Often this is go, no-go, pass-fail gauge or a win-loss measure. Such is the case of the baseball batter. Worth is measured at a point farther still. Most notably, worth is measured at the **point of use**. Economic attributes are common, visible and calculable at that point.

Those interested in monetizing information valuations must pay close attention to the measurement placement or they will think that this method is incomplete. The monetary units exist at the point of exchange and only there. This is a measurement dilemma for some. It is not a method flaw.

Measurement and Metrics - General

Applications of energy's Second Law provide crisp rules concerning process measures and metrics. We have illustrated the form many times but not specifically pointed it out. Magic measurement units take the form of $^{Output}/_{Input}$.

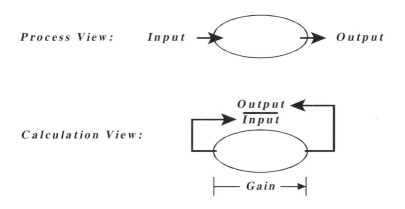

This is more difficult to explain than do. Here are examples:

$$\frac{Output}{Input} \left\{ \frac{\frac{Return}{Investment}}{\frac{Return}{Cost}} \quad \frac{\frac{Ending\ State}{Beginning\ State}}{\frac{Certainty}{Uncertainty}} \quad \frac{Goal}{Distance\ Away} \right\} \frac{Output}{Input}$$

A noteworthy distinction is that the measures (particularly return) are just outside the process. The measures exist at the **edge** of the process. Differences are measured in this manner.

The measurement positioning of an information process is hopefully clarified. The input is a level of uncertainty about something plus some (new) data plus the synthesis process. The synthesis process merges the previous knowledge (both familiarity and the gap of uncertainty) and rationalizes the ingredients so as to either reduce or not the uncertainty. The aim and the measure of the output in this case is the <u>degree of the state change reduction of uncertainty</u>.   This is what information is and this is what we intend to measure.

When this happens, the "whatever object" (person, system, enterprise) is more certain as the result. Measure of the differential information process change can be accomplished by testing before versus after or by tracking the performance differences in repeated time intervals.

Often we call this learning. The "whatever" learned something new. Whatever name, the event that has happened is information acquisition. Information moments happened. No economic consequence is necessarily evident although a potential may be estimated. The actual economic value is resolved at the **point of use** which may be immediate or long delayed. Thus, latency of use may defer and diffuse the economic realization. The information process can unconditionally claim to bias (change probabilities of) certain action paths after the information event as opposed to prior.

The difference created is an **information difference**. Detection and measurement of information is in the path variation. Economic impact is measured subsequently as the consequence of the informational variation.

The first step is to select a measuring scale. What we would like to have as a measure is some calculation function having the following properties:

1.   The measure would calculate and scale information content in all situations discrete and continuous (comprehensive).

2.   The measure should indicate that less certainty is present as the number of equally likely choices goes up (the three ball example).

3.   The measure should permit big choices to be separated into multiple staged sets of successive choices but the overall measure of certainty should be equal (a large collective uncertainty).

Point three above is the holistic versus reductionistic scenario. What it means is that the measure of one big uncertainty that has, for example, twelve (12) subordinate uncertainties should result in the same measure as the combined twelve (12) part uncertainty. The amount of information to resolve should be cumulative in exactly the same measuring sense. The decomposed uncertainties should equal the total.

Probability as a Measurement? Not Quite!

Although probability is tightly linked to uncertainty, the use of probability as THE information scale breaks down. Here is how and why that happens. The universal $^{Output}/_{Input}$ measures (page 96) always work. The requirement, however, is to know the **number of units** (the quantity) of input and output. The $^{Certainty}/_{Uncertainty}$ measure should have alerted that "something" is peculiar. Probability is not a unit quantity term.

We are now aimed at the problem issue. What are the **number of information content units** that are required to change a state of probability?

Expressions of (p) and/or (1-p) cannot be used as units to describe themselves. They are beginning and ending states. Something else must be the **number of units**. Otherwise, we end up in silly or nonsense scenarios as described below.

Certainty		Uncertainty (1/Certainty)
Half Certain	*(.5)*	*1/.5 = 2.0*
Three Quarter Certain	*(.75)*	*1/.75 = 1.3*
Fully Certain	*(1.0)*	*1/1.0 =* (1.0) ←*PROBLEM*

OOPS! If 100 percent certain then we need to be zero uncertain!

This Needs To Be Zero.

The only mathematical relationship (in all of science) that satisfies the condition which we desire for the information scale is the logarithmic function discovered by Boltzmann and **shown** by Shannon in communication theory.

Before considering the scale of information consider characteristics of the other types of measuring scales.

Physical descriptions somehow help get started. The scaling of information is very much like a thermometer. Consider the two scales of common thermometers.

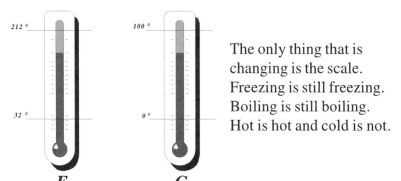

The only thing that is changing is the scale. Freezing is still freezing. Boiling is still boiling. Hot is hot and cold is not.

One of the similarities is the (confusing but convertible) change in the size of units and the position of "zero" in Fahrenheit measure versus Centigrade. The changing of numbering system basis introduces the "conversion" type confusion. It is quite okay to stick with one. They are convertible back and forth. BUT, for comparison the same one must be used. If one person is talking Centigrade and the other Fahrenheit, bad results are likely.

The other similarity is the fact that thermometers are measuring something invisible. Thermometers are measuring the evidence of energy content or lack of it. Heat is invisible to us. We can never see it. We "know" heat exists. The balance scale was actually measuring gravity differences between objects. Gravity is invisible. What we see is the evidence of heat and gravity. Evidence is information.

It is the scale that gives visibility. Notice that the same confusion and conversion problems exist between pounds and grams. No problem, pick one. All that happened was that different valuable people learned different valuable things at different points in time-place-space and **transported** their informational observations to us. It was BIG "news" at the time. We enjoy the consequences or are inflicted by them whichever side you want to view.

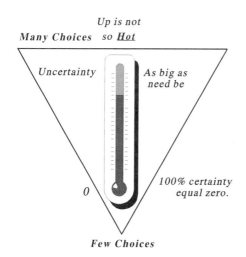

The scale of uncertainty which we want to use is fixed at zero but variable in the middle. What changes is the size of the problem and the units in the middle (for each problem situation).

We must do this because of the massive numbers of choices and the variety of situations.

Each situation has a scale, the same scale and one of two formulations depending on whether the situation is continuous (like the thermometer) or whether it is discrete (like the balance scale). The size of the units is going to be labeled H or S (just like F or C in temperature).[22]

Once this is accomplished we can measure the quantity of information content. What we have is the equivalent of the amount of cool content on a thermometer. It will be the amount of "not so hot" information.

The economic value of cool information requires the transfer to another measuring system, the economic exchange system. Fortunately, the economic exchange system works exactly the same way. Therefore, we can equate the information scale to the economic scale. Refer to associative measures in the literature or Appendix A.

---

[22]   Nomenclature. The authors are not enthused by the choice of notation used in the upcoming equations. This is the point of the scales. It would only add confusion however to make W=C=Choices.

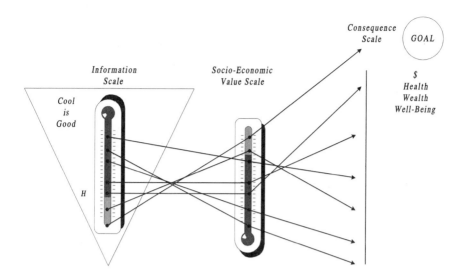

Given these desires for measuring information uncertainty, the only formulation in science that simultaneously satisfies the criteria is Ludwig Boltzmann's famous H theorem of entropy.

$$H = - K \Sigma P_i \ log \ P_i \qquad (\ Discrete \ Form)$$

$$S = K \ log \ W \qquad (\ Continuous \ Form)$$

$$
\begin{aligned}
Where \quad H \ &= S = Entropy \\
W \ &= Number \ of \ Choices \\
P_i \ &= Event \ Probability \\
&\quad Log \ can \ be \ any \ base \\
K \ &= Constant \ for \ log \ base \ conversion
\end{aligned}
$$

Both expressions above represent related forms of what is known in thermodynamics as entropy. In the physical sciences, the entropy associated with a situation is a measure of the degree of randomness, confusion or of "shuffledness" in the situation and the tendency of physical systems to become more and more perfectly shuffled.

The imbedded natural law is so fundamental that it is this tendency which gives time its arrow. It was Sir Arthur Eddington, the English physicist, who observed that the perception of whether a movie of the physical world is being run forward or backward is a consequence of the law.

It perhaps seems surprising and somewhat strange that the logarithm term is a part. One may recall that logarithms allow for the transferal between numbering systems—communication systems. It is accepted now that logarithmic measures are in fact the natural ones.

This small expression is the confluence and unification point where physical objects, communication, information, and energy intersect. This is ground zero for switching from the physical world to the symbolic information world. Consider that the range of application includes breaking secret information coding during World War II for the radar which perhaps saved England, for the telephone system, for steam engines, automobile engines and economic engines of enterprises and nations. The Return on Investment of financial analysis is entropy based.

The Information Advantage points out that the "scale of the solution instrument must match the magnitude of the problem." We have attempted to show the pervasive scope of information. The measuring methodology must be sufficiently broad to cover the entire scope of information. This one does. It is both exciting and amazing that it is so simple and elegant as to be expressed in a dozen simple symbols.

For convenience we will perform the computations and present the results in tabular and graphic form. Notice that the "zero problem" mentioned earlier is corrected. When there is but one choice remaining the uncertainty is zero.

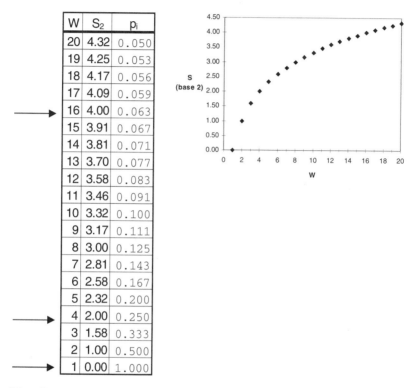

W	S_2	p_i
20	4.32	0.050
19	4.25	0.053
18	4.17	0.056
17	4.09	0.059
16	4.00	0.063
15	3.91	0.067
14	3.81	0.071
13	3.70	0.077
12	3.58	0.083
11	3.46	0.091
10	3.32	0.100
9	3.17	0.111
8	3.00	0.125
7	2.81	0.143
6	2.58	0.167
5	2.32	0.200
4	2.00	0.250
3	1.58	0.333
2	1.00	0.500
1	0.00	1.000

The figure and tabulations indicate information measurement in a base 2 binary measuring system. Shown is the connection between the numbers of choices (W), blind choice probability (P_i) and uncertainty (S). This scale of (S) is our scale of certainty or uncertainty (information). The latter portion of Appendix A develops a multidimension view.

This configuration may be thought of as representing the situation where queries or measuring instruments take the form yes or no, zero (0) or one (1), pass or fail, go or no-go. The "S" numbers are the information content "units" that we were missing a few pages earlier.

Shown at the top of this chart is the case where there are 20 choices (balls) and in this case uniform random probability is 0.05 for each. The uncertainty measure is 4.32 units. At the bottom of the list is one choice, the probability is 1.0 and the uncertainty is zero.

This matches our measurement criteria list. As more equal choices enter, the uncertainty is greater. The "S" scale works!

Notice that the curve is not a straight line (linear). For example, the 20 choice uncertainty is not twice the 10 choice uncertainty. Recall earlier when additions multiplied? Additional choices carry disproportionally less weight. What this implies is that once one doesn't know something, knowing less about the unknown isn't much worse.

A very powerful simple feature of the chart relating to problem solving and uncertainty resolution is imbedded in the "S" column.

What the "S" column calculates is the **minimum** number of yes-no questions that would be required to **guarantee** certainty. This is the relationship to the amount of missing information. Fractional yes-no items do not make much sense in this context so consider the "S's" which are whole numbers. In the case of two (2) choices exactly one yes/no question is required. In the case of four choices, two questions will resolve the issue and in the case of sixteen (16) it will take four (4).

One might consider that the **power** of the measuring instrument is connected to how rapidly the uncertainty can be resolved. The cost will relate to the energy investment per repetition of the instrumentation.

Consider our red, white, blue ball example. For W=3 the uncertainty is 1.58. This means that two yes/no questions will be required at a minimum to **guarantee** finding the "right" ball. Luck can happen but it is not guaranteed!

The information engineer may observe that a binary, yes/no instrument is not best for resolving the "3" choice case. If there existed a **three way resolver**, the three ball situation could be resolved in **one** query.

The three way case requires an identical computation with a simple change in base and this has been accomplished in the following chart and graphic.

W	S_3	p_i
20	2.73	0.050
19	2.68	0.053
18	2.63	0.056
17	2.58	0.059
16	2.52	0.063
15	2.46	0.067
14	2.40	0.071
13	2.33	0.077
12	2.26	0.083
11	2.18	0.091
10	2.10	0.100
9	2.00	0.111
8	1.89	0.125
7	1.77	0.143
6	1.63	0.167
5	1.46	0.200
4	1.26	0.250
3	1.00	0.333
2	0.63	0.500
1	0.00	1.000

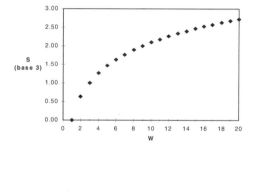

An instrument that resolves three way queries is a normal balance scale. People often mistake it for a two way device. However, consider in our earlier red, white, blue example that the "right" ball was known to be heavier. Placing **any two balls** on the scale will completely resolve the uncertainty.

Notice that in all the discussion concerning the balls and most everything else we show exactly how to find the "right" object without ever mentioning or knowing which is the right one. It is an information process power thing . . . powerful.

A 10 way physical object weight resolution device might be something that looks like a wagon wheel scale.

All items or all except one could be placed at the spoke points and the heavy object would be resolved. Balancing auto wheels works this way so that the wheels do not VIBRATE later.

The diagram for the base numbering system which we use most (ten) is shown below.

W	S_{10}	p_i
20	1.30	0.050
19	1.28	0.053
18	1.26	0.056
17	1.23	0.059
16	1.20	0.063
15	1.18	0.067
14	1.15	0.071
13	1.11	0.077
12	1.08	0.083
11	1.04	0.091
10	1.00	0.100
9	0.95	0.111
8	0.90	0.125
7	0.85	0.143
6	0.78	0.167
5	0.70	0.200
4	0.60	0.250
3	0.48	0.333
2	0.30	0.500
1	0.00	1.000

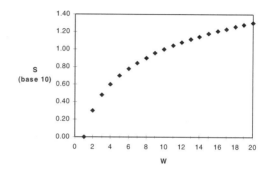

The gist of the rule says that there exists an uncertainty re-solver[23] instrument the power of which equals the numbering system base of the logarithm. The amount of uncertainty which can be accomplished in a given incidence (turn of the crank) is equal to the size of resolving power (information acquisition bits) of the instrument. Complete resolution to certainty then takes the number of repeated turns as calculated by S (or H which is equivalent).

[23]   Ahead of Time dramatically expands on this feature relative to business optimization.

Lost at Sea

This is the first opportunity to analyze the friend lost at sea with the information measurement method. Recall (from page 16) that one friend, five passengers and thirty crew went out. The message came in, "one **person** lost." The various numeric information content measurement descriptions are shown below following the procedure just presented.

Odds	Friend Probability	Information Content (Base 2)	Information Content (Base 10)
35 to 1	1/36	5.2	1.6

Then a second "new" message arrived indicating the lost person was a **passenger**. New information creates new probabilities. When the final answer is known the uncertainty will be zero (0). That has not yet happened (to these participants).

Odds	Friend Probability	Information Content (Base 2)	Information Content (Base 10)
5 to 1	1/6	2.6	.8

The difference[24] in content or the amount of content difference is consistently 50 percent reduction of uncertainty regardless of the logarithmic base upon which the computations are made. Next, we will explain where to find the baseline and why.

---

[24] Notice that if one were to use probabilities or odds it would be very difficult to see that there is 50 percent content difference between 35 to 1 and 5 to 1. The "statistics" being presented here are NOT the same as typical statistics. Refer to Appendix A Comments.

Literal Temperature Scale

Readers should not take the thermometer scale and analogy too literally. The measurement scale does not necessarily imply absolute zero Kelvin temperature. It could. The relationship has a closer affinity to "time" as expressed by Sir Eddington and to combinatorial mathematics.

The "zero" point of the scale is merely the point where one choice resolves the uncertainty to zero. Sometimes ten things can be resolved to zero in one choice, sometimes more, sometimes less.

Measuring and Calculating Information Power

Recall earlier when we mentioned the normal "C" and the exemplary "B" corporation or workgroup.

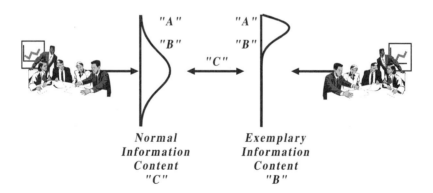

Normal
Information
Content
"C"

Exemplary
Information
Content
"B"

The **secret** that scientists, statisticians and teachers don't tell is that the "normal" distribution is the WORST business case. This distribution possesses the ugly characteristic of possessing the lowest capacity to perform work. Technically, this distribution is **guaranteed** to have the highest entropy (not good) and least collective information content (twice not good).

This may be good news, bad news or no news at all. What evidently is news to many is that the formulation of measures and metrics for enterprise information content can be (and has been) formulated from this natural, scientific basis.

As with so many things it is quite simple. Here is how it works. Measurement systems require a scale and a metric of measure to determine the **space between** items. Achievement of this prerequisite allows the calculation of a value along the scale.

The fact that the Gaussian, or normal distribution, is the **worst** provides the valuable basis from which information goodness measures and metrics can be determined. What results is the relative information POWER of a group of objects.

The solution of information content is found in the measure of the degree of differential goal control exhibited by the system being measured. The logic is simple. We know from science that the only way to control a process or system is with information. Therefore, the lack of information (uncertainty) is evidenced, directly related and calculable as lack of control.

Everything has redeeming value in some frame. The virtue of ugly is that one then appreciates pretty. The virtue of worst being identified is that better and best become clearer. The BEST is found FARTHEST from worst on the scale (and vice versa).

A simple view may be the archer in <u>The Information</u> <u>Advantage</u>.

Consider a hoard of archers AIMING at a target with incentive to hit it.

Some hit, some miss and someone keeps score. How is the scoring done?

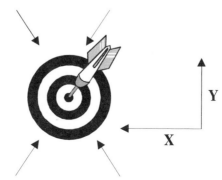

In two dimensions the resultant arrows may be high, low, left, right, high right, high left, low right, low left or just right. The measure of goodness in two dimensions is the distance from the bull's-eye. The distance is calculated by the length of the line from the target to each arrow.

$$d = \sqrt{X^2 + Y^2}$$

Most often **error** from uncontrol results in "normal" or normal-like distributions. In the case of two-dimensional target archery scoring, the distribution of "d" is "circular normal" which happens to be chi square like. The bull's-eye eliminates one tail of a customary normal. The distribution is biased toward the target center. The larger point here is the position of the target at the extreme end, rather than the average. An explicit ordering has occurred to position "best" far away from both average and worst.

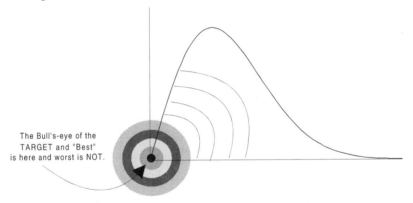

The Bull's-eye of the TARGET and "Best" is here and worst is NOT.

In three dimensions the problem is still the same but time is often the third dimension.

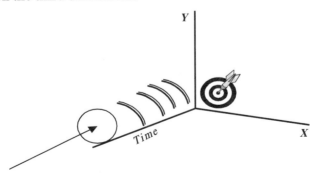

The scorer takes a snapshot of the arrow while it is in the air heading toward the target and scores where it is going to hit. The scorer moves the "window" of opportunity outward and calculates the degree of control. Radar works this way. It was mentioned earlier that "best" is exclusive but not necessarily singular. There are any number of arrow arcs that know how to hit the target.

Consider the control information connection. Consider that the archer cannot "see" the target . . . no information. The arrows will be launched rather randomly with wide variance — little control. Consider that the archer has not accounted for wind or other critical (valuable) parameters. This is missing information — lack of control.

The fact that some archers reliably hit the target with precision is evidence that they possess relatively superior information. Information permits the archer to control the outcome.

In particular the measure here is one of EFFECTIVENESS. The aiming (guidance) process (and everything behind it) is being measured as the degree of control in targeting. The expression "where comes before how" epitomizes this activity. In business this measure is attributed to the enterprise executive or management control information. Later, we will calculate the measure of management control information in a real enterprise situation.

Efficiency is **not present** in this example. One might suspect that the "winning" archer did not put more energy into the arrow's release. The bull's-eye requires the just right choices. The "production information," the choices previous to launch, determines the efficiency.

The only data[25] required for the computation were the goal and
the actual results. The other archers, the "hoard," did not add
to the measure except in the relative sense and perhaps in the
economic context. If there happened to be a large economic
outcome for the "winner," then the information becomes
economically viable also.

Economic payoff happens after the outcome event and is
measured in economic terms (a change in scale). This is a next
process linkage in reality and likewise a next process step in
the calculation. The accomplishment is the same. Recall that
the measure was to be taken at the input and output edge of the
process. If one extends the process then there are new edges.

Contribution to Variance - Explanation and Consequences[26]

Control of variation IS process control. Information process
conforms but is a bit convoluted. Keep in mind that variation
is a pattern of difference. This is information. The study of
process control is the study of the kinds of variation that can
occur, the sources of these variances and the means, methods
and practices by which variances can be managed.

The measure of <u>effectiveness</u> of process control is the degree to
which variances are minimized relative to the output target.
Process control efficiency then is the amount of information
energy utilized to achieve a given level (or coordination) of
variation in the resulting output.

---

[25]   Notice what was **not required** for the measure. All the decisions, the energy, the
practicing, the diet of the archer, the cost history, and all the "impossibles" were not
required.

[26]   ANOVA: Analysis of Variance is a statical interpretation of variance. Here we are
interpreting the deeper information and control aspects.

In repeated processes such as those found in business the repeated measure will form a distribution of observations. The mean of the distribution, the standard deviation and the performance standard are of interest.

The difference between the <u>mean</u> and the intended target is a measure of how close a process is to satisfying the target. It is a measure of the <u>accuracy</u> of a process. The <u>standard deviation</u>, as a measure of dispersion, indicates the degree to which a process is capable of <u>repeating</u> the targeted performance. The smaller the dispersion, the more capable the process is of repeating the desired performance. This is the information content measure. The process "knows." It is a measure of <u>precision</u> and is constrained or not in the ability of the participating elements to repeat identical performance. <u>Repeatability</u> may be due to people, machines, procedures or whatever. Often the variance due to people and procedures is termed <u>reproducibility, a synonym of repeatability.</u>

The "Vibes"[27]

Recall the vibrations given off in the process diagram earlier. The following are the informational meanings.

Recall a few pages earlier when the 10-way static wheel balancer was used to eliminate future VIBRATIONS. These are the types of dynamic "vibes" which are the signaling information when forward time becomes "now."

Upon repeated measures over time for measured events it occurs that the mean of the process keeps changing. The standard deviation of the mean of the process, defined as the <u>stability</u> of the process is a measure of how well it performs over time. System <u>variance</u> is the net composite variance due to accuracy, precision, reproducibility and stability.

---

[27]   The business and social consequence and connection among the linkages of information, variance and entropy was first discovered by James Thoreson (<u>The Information Advantage</u>) and analytically explained by John Blankenship.

Stability

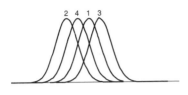

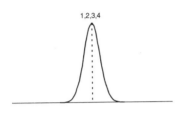

The smaller the variance of the mean of a process (or its square root which is the standard deviation of the mean), the more stable is the process over time.

The information in the top system is not sufficiently intense or powerful to prevent variation in the mean. The bottom system possesses fewer choices, lower entropy and more control.

Accuracy

Time 1

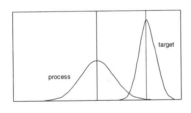

This is a pattern example of accuracy. Note the target remains the same and the process mean is moving over time closer to the target or goal.

Time 2

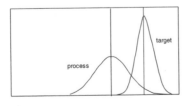

The process is making dynamic adjustments and therefore is also demonstrating adaptability. Feedback information is present.

Time 3

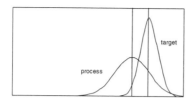

Information in the system is improving over time toward achieving the target. Learning is evident in the sense of making more appropriate choices towards target.

Time Dynamics

Consider that rather than the target being fixed (static) that each graphic represents a time snapshot where the target is also moving. Relative to the target the image is identical.

Precision

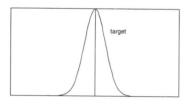

This is an example of precision. The dispersion or variance of the process is narrowing to more closely match the target distribution.

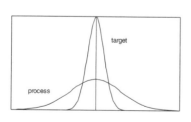

Note, however, that this second pattern may be more versatile than the lower pattern thus suggesting conflicting characteristics between precision and versatility. This is akin to the generalist versus specialist scenario.

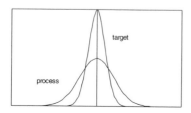

Information is improving relative to the target. The production variance is reduced.

Accuracy, as earlier noted, is the systematic bias in a process and stability is the manner in which the bias shifts over time. To the extent that process controls cause proper alteration, the information bias alters outcomes to bring results closer to the targeted outcome.

The capability of a process to make dynamic adjustments and correct for unwarranted information bias is termed adaptability. A measure of adaptability is the variance between the system variance and variance in repeatability.

Versatility is the ability of a process to accommodate variety. Variety may come in the form of specifications, methods, machine types, people backgrounds, skills or whatever. Greater versatility often reflects greater complexity and the contributing factors to variance can be expected to increase. Versatility infers a wide **range** of information.

The interpretation and analysis of contribution to variance must carefully consider the process design intention. For example, the requirement for adaptability is quite different to produce one result versus producing a large number of identical sequential results (parts). To be successful with a single unique occurrence a process must possess a high degree of accuracy. For large numbers of serially repeated occurrences precision and stability are more critical because adjustments can compensate for accuracy. Information design criteria need be selected to accomplish each. The greater the stability of a process, the less frequently it will need adjustment.

We hope to have clarified the relationship between information and variation. Information is **the** contributor. Accuracy, precision, and reproducibility characteristics of a process each result from differing conditions of cause. The cause is always information related.[28]

---

[28]   The Information Advantage, op. cit., p. 279. All cause is informational at the root.

The techniques of control required to manage (minimize) the variation in each type variation are not equal .... in fact they are quite different. Enterprises find it difficult and confusing to simultaneously manage the conflicting demands of several apparently conflicting control structures.

The monetizing of information worth directly follows the variation analysis related to the choice of metrics used to form the $^{Output}/_{Input}$ process statistic. A common terminology is Return on Investment. The accuracy and precision of Return on Investment might be represented by the previously shown distribution forms. The adaptiveness and precision would then represent the information value in achieving stable, increasing ROI. Examples in the next section further illustrate.

Measurement Consequence

The energy to create the "waves" shown in the previous pages is happening continuously. This is what information entropy is. The data is present whether or not it is measured. Like the riddle of the tree falling in the forest,[29] the consequence of not listening and turning the data into information may be severe.

Extra measurement (beyond measuring the original waves) in order to be valid removes a bit of energy from the object being measured thus changing its energy state. This makes a differ-ence (which is information) in the outcome as opposed to what would have been and thus the information from the measuring ends up changing the original system outcome slightly. This is another form of bias. Measurement has changed the outcome and made a difference. We term this the cost of "control." This is the cost of coordinating directed outcomes. "News" changes outcomes but extracts a price in the doing.

---

[29]   ibid, pp. 317 - 320.

Control is the Key

It is really quite simple. What one MUST KNOW and believe is that information (in some dimension or form) is the singular determinate for directed (controlled) action. This should not be "news" because it is proven in science. The only, only, only . . . (a thousand onlys) way to control the direction of an outcome of anything is with some form of information. Period.

Therefore, it follows that if something is not perfectly controlled or exhibits properties of lack of control then the thing that **is lacking** is **always** some form of **information**. The amount of information missing is equal to a measurement of the degree of uncontrol . . . the uncertainty.

In nature perfectly random is equally as difficult to achieve as perfectly perfect. Neither is an achievable natural state. Nature does not allow perfection to be a stable event state. Period! Nature is perfectly non-perfect.

If any one thing could be made perfectly deterministic then that would lead to others and control would be imposed and so on until time would stop. Everything would be frozen rigid. Absolutely nothing would ever happen afterward (absolute zero).

Perfectly equal probabilities in the case of discrete events and perfectly no variance in the case of continuous distributions are the perfection points from which information content can be measured. In actuality they are the same. Discrete points are merely (static) points on the (dynamic) continuum where time has been momentarily, artificially (unnaturally) stopped to measure.

The Chaos Connection — Structure and Coherence

Work and heat are distinct in the sense that work is the transfer of energy as coherent motion and heat is energy transfer as incoherent motion. Throughout we have shown work as a process, a method and not a "thing." According to our definitional direction (the dynamic rethinking), work is now a structure too. This is the case because of the decision to identify coherence with structure, whatever form the coherence may take. Structure and coherence are synonyms. What is not quite as obvious is that structure defines the range[30] of coherence from greater to lesser (to include constructive chaos as well as destructive chaos).

The idea that structure signifies coherence with orderly and stable arrangements, whereas lack of structure signifies incoherent willy-nilly arrangement, neatly captures solids as structures but allows gases to escape as structureless. These are structures in space, spatial structures.

Another dimension of structure was introduced that included coherence over time. The periodic cycle of events over time shows patterns of time oriented structures.

Nature has an extraordinary time nonuniform way of slipping into chaos. It does so unevenly. The picture here is like the ragged surface of the rapids. Every so often, even in the rapids, there is a local area of smoothness where the chaos disappears into calm. The world does not degenerate monotonously uniformly.

---

[30]   ibid, pp. 150-151.

The structure of change and the information about it is the outcome of the clashes of purposeless operations of chaos. So long as a process is occurring in which more chaos is generated than is being destroyed, then the balance of the energy may be withdrawn as coherent motion (work). This statement may seem striking but it too is The Second Law. Coherent local structure emerges if (and only if) it is coupled to a greater disorder. Such is the power of the Boltzmann formula. Recall the formula S=k log W. This equation exactly describes the manner in which chaos governs **direction** and the **rate** of chaotic exchanges. The world of appearance, information and distillations of experience (knowledge) is represented by "S." The left side term, "S", is the visible part of the exchange which we observe. On the right hand side is the offsetting entry which must be there but may or may not be visible. It may be in the future or may have already happened. It may be near or far away. In any event, it is real and really happens.

Consider what happens to a drop of ink when placed into a beaker of clear water. Information behaves this way. Over time the ink distributes itself rather uniformly throughout the water changing its color content. There is nothing (except probability) to prevent the ink from reforming into the original, cohesive drop. Once a new state has been achieved, as in the world of experience, the universe is locked out of the past. Any turning back is simply too improbable. Now consider dropping in a clear ink with the same color as the water. What happens?

This is the basis of our measuring scale. The measurement of the information content of dissipative structures is the certainty with which each combats uncertainty.

7. EXAMPLE MEASURES

Supply Chain Example

A most challenging, fun, exciting and frustrating experience exists in supply chain management. The famous MIT "Beer Game"[31] is an excellent simulation. A most interesting phenomenon occurs as part of the exercise. The supply chain participants can function well individually but cannot collectively perform.

The net result is what Thoreson[32] terms an "uncertainty avalanche."

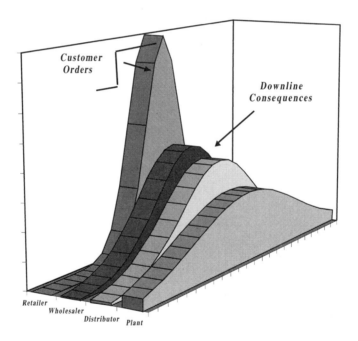

---

[31]   John D. Sterman, "Modeling Managerial Behavior: Misperceptions of Feedback In A Dynamic Decision Making Experiment," Sloan School of Management, Massachusetts Institute of Technology, March 1989, also Peter M. Senge, The Fifth Discipline, 1990.

[32]   The Information Advantage, op.cit., pp. 479-491.

The economic consequence in the simulation is approximately the difference between $40,000 and $40. The consequence in business is similarly significant.

Constructs of Competitiveness

Baseball

In contentious systems, sometimes termed dissipative systems, multiple participants are striving for a commonly sought aim. In the student example the aim is an "A" but not all achieve it (by design?). In the reliability example the aim is perfect success (1.0 reliability) or the alternative of zero failures. In the baseball batter case the aim might be to reach one or more bases safely 40 percent of the time (.400). In each case obstacles (competitors) stand in the path of accomplishment.

Bridge

Stochastic, dynamic, competitive structures (games) were originally developed to investigate the mathematics and dynamics of uncertainty. Games and other sorts of simulators remain as good examples and good practicing.

An information entropy content analysis of the card game of bridge may aid the reader in appreciating information power computations.

We will use the standard point system here to demonstrate. Recall that in a hand (yours) Ace=4 points, King=3 points, Queen=2 points, etc. These numerical values are assigned so that additions and subtractions in scoring are possible.

The distribution of points of possible hands in the deck before it is dealt approximately follows the pattern of the normal distribution. This distribution is shown below:

Point Distribution

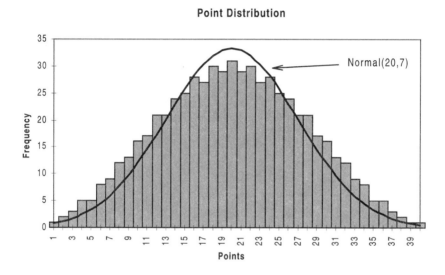

One might think of the bridge points system rather like "assets" in business financial accounting. The more powerful high worth assets have higher values because they are high probability "winners." Similarly, the partners' hands synergize (or not) and combine assets from the pool of possibilities against the opponents' pool.

After receiving a specific hand from the distribution of possibilities the participants score their individual hand.

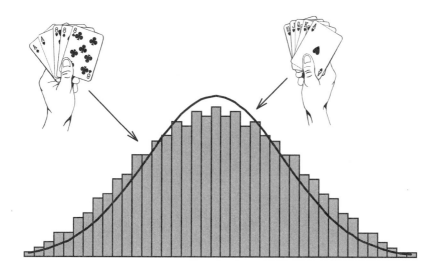

Grading Curve

Recall the school grading system. The hands fall into information power categories.

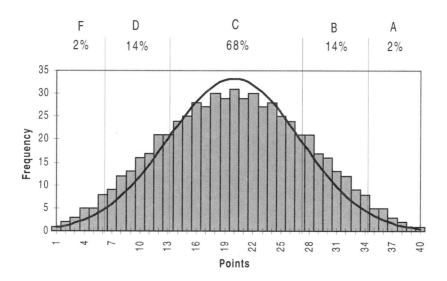

The team partners' hands synergize together (or not). The team that possesses the more powerful information advantage is in a better position to win.

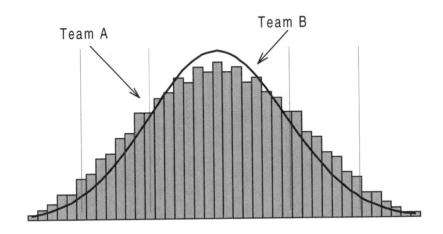

Frighteningly Large Numbers

The barrier arises in the apparent large numbers created by combinatorial mathematics. For example, with as few as three variables, each having ten choices, there are 10 x 10 x 10 or 1,000 possible combinations. If analyzing each of these choices takes ten hours, then ten thousand (10,000) hours would be required by the assessment.

A card deck of 52 cards is often dealt among 4 players (such as for bridge). In these cases each of the 4 receivers end up with 13 cards.

There are more than 635 billion (635,000,000,000) possible combinations for the 13 cards. The challenge of finding a "final contract" among the choices only takes a few minutes. The process to accomplish this is obviously learnable and simple. One need not be intimidated by large numbers.

Once the hands are dealt, the billions of possibilities reduce to just a few. In bridge, there are but thirty-six contract possibilities. Given a contract, the outcome is even simpler. The contract holding team either produces at or above the level specified in the contract — win or lose.

The simplifying rule that the masters use is "where comes before how." Masters solve the problem backwards.[33] They step ahead in time and examine the possible outcomes (thirty-six bids) versus the billions of possibilities. Situational choices are considered relative to vulnerability and distribution of cards held. Each card is then an asset or a constraint in the range of enhancing to destructive. This is rather like assets and liabilities.

It is noteworthy that collaboration is required to determine the synergy of "assets" between partners against the competition. The form of this collaboration is an information exchange with a very restricted vocabulary zero (pass), one, two, three, four, five, six, seven, no trump, spades, hearts, diamonds or clubs. *Double*, *redouble* and *review* complete the bridge vocabulary set. The rules (informational) control the boundaries of the activity and restrict the information exchange. The score of effectiveness (win-lose) is determined outside the process.

---

[33] In Operations Research a technique entitled dynamic programming instructs the solving of problems backwards. The advantage is the immediate elimination of large numbers of nonoptimal path choices.

Bellman, Richard: Some applications of the Theory of Dynamic Programming - A Review, Journal of the Operations Research Society of America, vol. 2, no. 3 August, 1954, as well as various other publications on dynamic programming.

Instructional Example — Top Gun

The "Top Gun" training in military aviation is an excellent example. We do not possess the actual data for Top Gun training during its war years inception and subsequent development. As such this scenario is transitionally attempting to illustrate the techniques.

The training addresses not only life and death survival (asset protection, defense) but, as a dual consequence, addresses success enhancement (offense, winning). The information in the training satisfies the requirement for valuable information.

The best choices of goal metric (system aim) are ones that exhibit a wide range (scale) of outcome possibilities. For example here, the Top Gun scale ranges from high success to failure and death. The authors doubt that the government is aware of the science behind Top Gun. Despite the unawareness of the specific founding science, the system sought and found a competitive edge.

The choice of effectiveness metrics upon which to base the measures is quite critical and delicate. The diagram on page 94 should be of assistance. Part of the search for proper measures is the notion that the aim is positioned outside the system being measured but all participants are aware of its existence, importance and usually the computation. That is, the metric is very visible and obvious, sometimes to the point of extreme simplicity. In the case of Top Gun, the measurement is based on the morbid but necessary "kill ratio." Notice that the real effectiveness of the school is measured not at the school but when the new information is put to use. Information is transportable and the measure of value is separated widely from the receipt incidence.

The calculation of information content for the entire group of Top Gun participants would be accomplished with the activities described in Appendix A.

As time goes forward and more and more success happens, the measurement trend will flow as illustrated below.

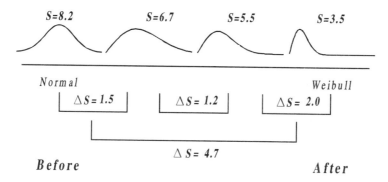

The economic value of the information transfer will then be calculated conventionally. This will include the difference in equipment lost, the amount of enemy damage difference and so on.

Educational Institutions

It does take practice to develop meaningful constructs. In addition, the data are moderately difficult to acquire.

A different viewpoint may be of greater interest to directors of training (or universities). Consider much the same scenario as that in industry. The objective of the assessment is to determine the information assimilation rate (the competency achievement rate).

The method of what would need to be done to measure the real value might be instructive in considering that the objective is to measure the economic value of the information transferred.

The method would entail constructing a sampling of students graduating from the university over their subsequent lifetime. Each year each student, or a significant sample, would respond with their income and or net worth statement.

Other universities or departments within a single university might also participate.

A second distribution would be formed from those students not attending at all and/or those attending one of the "other" participating universities.

The methodology would yield the comparative results.

Some universities do this now.

Reliability, Value Case

This case is intended to describe an integrated scenario involving process, reliability, value, information, and profit engineering disciplines. We will step through the problem solving stages of a hypothetical business named XYZ Corporation. The structure of the explanation separates the executive team chronology from the technical aspects and computations. Group working sessions are described here. Individual computational (off-line) work matches the sequence, but is presented in Appendix B.

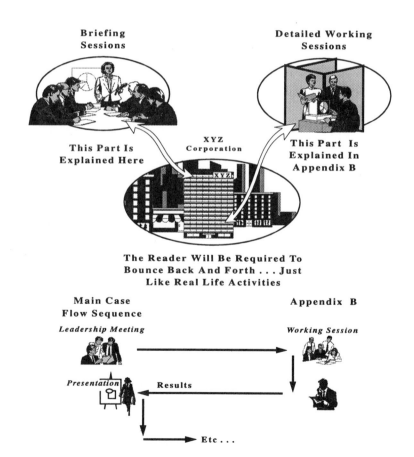

Background

XYZ Corp. has been in business for some time and produces an attractive, but somewhat perishable, marketplace offering. The exact type of object is not pertinent to this case.

The CEO (Dave) has had the insight to expose and train all staff in process (Quality) doctrines, and XYZ personnel have generally been successful in implementing small process improvements. They understand process basics.

The CFO (June) is under constant pressure for profitability. The remainder of the execu-tive and supervisory team is interested in improvement also. All agree that major im-

provement is both possible and needed.

As they begin, the team explains that the critical process connects in a serial link as described below.

Base System

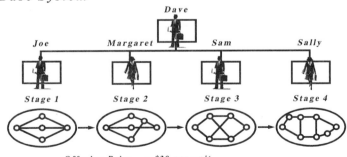

```
Offering Price   = $30 per unit
Production Rate  = 96 units/day
Repair Period    = 24 hours
Production Run   = 24 hours/day, 30 day/month
```

The system experiences several days of downtime a month. The downtime affects the amount of customer offerings that XYZ can produce and, therefore, has a negative impact on monthly operating performance.

The same component does not fail each time; however, when one component fails, all others are idle because of system dependencies. The conclusion of the group is that reliability of the system must be improved.

Operating

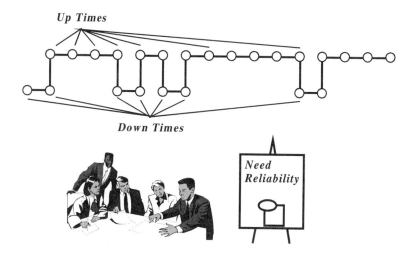

<u>*Reliability*</u>

The company assigns the task of examining the system for areas of improvement to two people: 1) a business process analyst and 2) a reliability engineer. Refer to B.1 for their work in the back office.

The inspection is done relative to the problem, and the reliability engineer speaks to the rest of the group about reliability at the executive session.

Reliability Engineer

"XYZ's business is a complex set of linkages, each dependent on the other. With this increased complexity, the number of functions performed, costs, and number of support facilities also rises. The complexity of these interrelated activities has caused a rise in maintenance costs and hence the need for reliable components and configurations."

"The reliability of any process depends on the number of and reliability of its component parts within each stage. Stage reliability can be achieved in only two ways:

1.   Decrease the failure rate of the individual components by improving the base items.

2.   Add redundant, parallel components."

"XYZ has the opportunity to control the levels of reliability to any degree practical through redundancy or individual component item reliability improvement. Its belief here is that it has the best possible component items and, therefore, needs to address redundancy."

"The driving issue behind reliability is using a **system view** of the process instead of the individual stages or components. It is critical to improve reliability using the entire system, because it is system reliability that needs to improve."

"Adding redundant components to areas with the lowest reliability does not practically optimize system reliability for discrete systems."

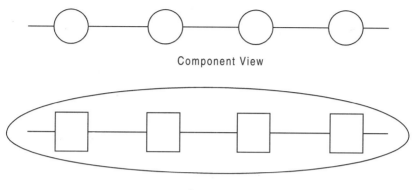

Component View

System View

"The base system at XYZ can be simplified to a serial system with one component per stage. The system reliability is dependent on the individual component reliability within each stage."

System 1

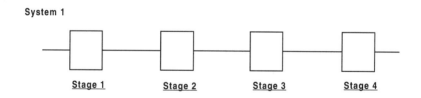

Stage 1   Stage 2   Stage 3   Stage 4

"Recall that we chose this configuration because it was the best cost. We needed at least one of each item and so that is what we did."

The reliability engineer goes on to explain that redundant components are required and shows an illustration.

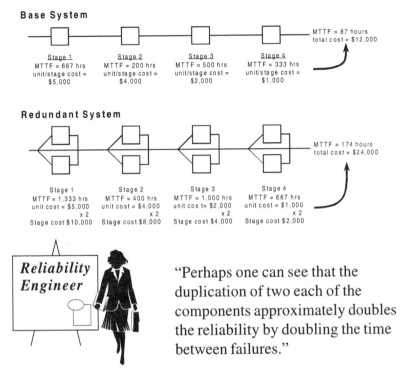

Base System

Stage 1
MTTF = 667 hrs
unit/stage cost =
$5,000

Stage 2
MTTF = 200 hrs
unit/stage cost =
$4,000

Stage 3
MTTF = 500 hrs
unit/stage cost =
$2,000

Stage 4
MTTF = 333 hrs
unit/stage cost =
$1,000

MTTF = 87 hours
total cost = $12,000

Redundant System

Stage 1
MTTF = 1,333 hrs
unit cost = $5,000
x 2
Stage cost $10,000

Stage 2
MTTF = 400 hrs
unit cost = $4,000
x 2
Stage cost $8,000

Stage 3
MTTF = 1,000 hrs
unit cos t= $2,000
x 2
Stage cost $4,000

Stage 4
MTTF = 667 hrs
unit cost = $1,000
x 2
Stage cost $2,000

MTTF = 174 hours
total cost = $24,000

Reliability Engineer

"Perhaps one can see that the duplication of two each of the components approximately doubles the reliability by doubling the time between failures."

The CFO questions whether the company can afford having double and/or triple units. More particularly, the question is relative to "What do we get?" . . . the answer is higher reliability.

Department heads, which are different for each of the stages, all volunteer to implement the redundancy in their area (if the company will give them the budget). Naturally each does not want to be the point of high failure.

The reliability engineer ends the meeting by explaining that various configurations can be constructed that offer choices in trade-offs between cost and reliability.

The session ends with a request to explore other configurations and return with two of the best choices. See Appendix B.2 for the off-line construction of choices.

Next Session - Decision

Having considered the various choices off-line (see Appendices B.1, B.2) the two "best" configurations are brought forward for choice.

Configuration 1 candidate has the following characteristics:

Configuration 1

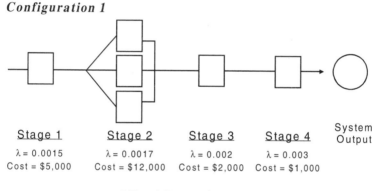

Stage 1	Stage 2	Stage 3	Stage 4	System Output
$\lambda = 0.0015$	$\lambda = 0.0017$	$\lambda = 0.002$	$\lambda = 0.003$	
Cost = $5,000	Cost = $12,000	Cost = $2,000	Cost = $1,000	

* Total Cost = $20,000
MTTF = 122 Hours

Configuration 2 candidate has the following characteristics:

Configuration 2

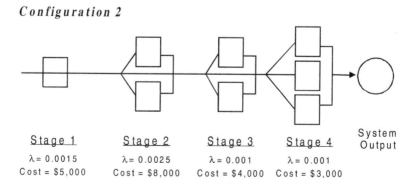

Stage 1	Stage 2	Stage 3	Stage 4	System Output
$\lambda = 0.0015$	$\lambda = 0.0025$	$\lambda = 0.001$	$\lambda = 0.001$	
Cost = $5,000	Cost = $8,000	Cost = $4,000	Cost = $3,000	

* Total Cost = $20,000
MTTF = 166 Hours

* See Appendix B for the analysis and calculation.

Which one to choose? No Problem! Configuration 2 has a superior failure rate than Configuration 1 for the same investment. On cue the financial allocation committee asks "What is the business impact?"

Here is what will happen. For the purpose of this example, it is known that the overall system creates four units per hour when the system is operating and the system requires 24 hours to repair each time it is broken. When no failures occur, the system operates 24 hours per day, 30 days per month. It is also known that all units made are sold at $30 per unit. When no failures occur and all units are sold, the system produces 96 units at a revenue of $2,880 per day or $86,400 per month.

The base system has a monthly operating cost of $12,000 and a failure rate of 0.0115, meaning the system fails nine (9) times per month. The system loses $25,920 revenue during those nine days, lowering the monthly revenue to $60,480. The profit for the base system per month is $48,480.

Configuration 2 costs $20,000, but it has a failure rate of 0.006. It fails five (5) times during the month, losing $14,400. The monthly revenue for Configuration 2 is $72,000, and it generates monthly profit of $52,000.

	Maximum Revenue (+)	Lost Revenue Due to Failures (-)	System Cost (-)	Monthly Profit =
Base	$86,400	$25,920	$12,000	$48,480
Configuration 2	$86,400	$14,400	$20,000	$52,000

Joe, who is the department manager of Stage 1, mumbles that his reliability is not being improved and why does Sally (stage 4) get two more redundant units and he gets none. Dave remarks something about teamwork. The project is approved and at the same time a discussion session on alignment is scheduled. The reliability engineer escorts Joe to the work room and shows him that the system would not be better if he received redundant units.

Alignment

Alignment Discussion—A System Viewpoint

The activities in each stage are in different interconnected work groups, separated physically (different buildings) and politically (different departments). Each department is judged by its individual failure-success rate. No one likes to be responsible for the failure.

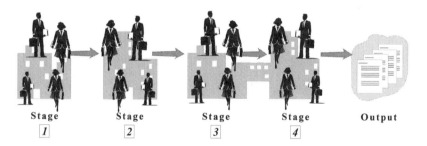

| Stage 1 | Stage 2 | Stage 3 | Stage 4 | Output |

In the absence of a system-wide view each department would contend for investment to increase its group's performance. This would make sense. Each of the managers would promote their individual interest. The "squeaky wheel" approach may or may not be appropriate. Although improvement would occur, the same investment produces higher results if configured to the system goal as opposed to the fragmented, separate group goals.

Dave explains to Joe, "Consider, Joe, that you and your group are so good as to not need more resource and expense. You are the highest Return on Investment group from a reliability point of view. The others need a "crutch." This makes Joe feel better.

The implementation occurs and so do the results. Dave schedules a celebration party.

At the party an information engineer (Barb) overhears the jubilation. She comments to Dave, "More could be done to improve profitability using the very same technique that solved the reliability problem if you wish."

"You mean reliability improvement?" responds Dave.

"No, you have already done that." says Barb.

"Do you mean Quality?" asks Dave, "Because, those are the two things that we have already done."

"No, you were actually doing a form of information engineering," explains Barb.

Dave responds, "Come in and present to us what you are talking about next week. Today, let's celebrate!" (The information engineer goes to work in preparation. Refer to B.3)

Next Week

XYZ knew from process training the INFORMATION to know how to begin looking at process opportunities and to make the choice that reliability needed to be investigated.

Barb says to the group:

"XYZ originally selected the
base configuration with one
unit each, because you had the
INFORMATION that at least
one unit was needed. Then,
you assumed that one unit
would be the least cost on the
basis that fewer are better.
How could you cut any more
costs?"

"From the list of choices the reliability engineer could choose
the single best configuration choice for gains in the reliability
goal. Information about the business impact of reliability
surfaced and you acted. This is good. The information helped.
I'm sure you now wish you had done it earlier."

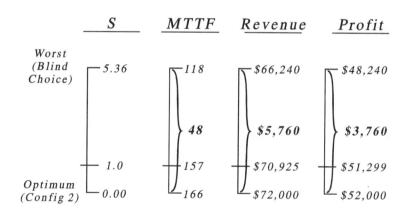

	S	*MTTF*	*Revenue*	*Profit*
Worst (Blind Choice)	5.36	118	$66,240	$48,240
		48	$5,760	$3,760
	1.0	157	$70,925	$51,299
Optimum (Config 2)	0.00	166	$72,000	$52,000

1 Unit of Information =   9 Hrs   (MTTF)

1 Unit of Information = $1,075 (Revenue)

1 Unit of Information = $ 701 (Profit)

"A blind choice from the list of possible configurations results in an uncertainty level of 5.36 and an average mean time to failure of 118 hours. Notice that any other random choice is better than the base case (MTTF = 87). The amount of information content difference that the reliability engineer resolved was 5.36. This equated to $5,760 positive difference in revenue and $3,760 positive difference in profitability. That was what the information was worth." Refer to Appendix B.3

"The next information you really need concerns customer preferences. I can see by your static pricing that there is an opportunity. It is uncertain whether you can capture the opportunity but it won't hurt to try because the returns are large. Have you rigorously analyzed price lately, or ever?" The group responds, "No."

Barb continues, "Do you realize that if you are charging too much or too little, you will also be losing profit? You should investigate value engineering. Value engineering works just like process engineering and reliability engineering. Information content makes a difference. The more certainty that XYZ corporation has about critical business control topics, the better off it is. What the project entails is determining the price demand profile so that we can price with certainty, as opposed to guessing. The activity gets started with Value Engineering. Do you want to consider it?" The group is reluctant but says, "Yes, have someone present an overview at the next session."

Value Engineering Session

A value engineer joins the group and requests a brief presentation on the events to this point. She speaks to the group about pricing:

"Configuring pricing is just like designing and configuring anything else. The only limitation is information. With your offering consider that a single price of $30 is very, very unlikely to fit the profile of your customers."

"Price is your way of controlling revenue and you are not exercising proper discipline for control. Your price looks stable but it is really 'tunable' just like reliability."

"No matter what price you choose there will be some that will gladly pay more and some will be turned off."

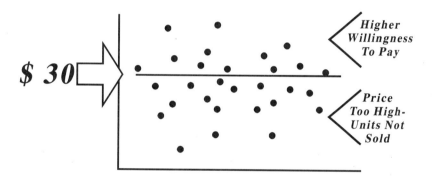

"If the dots here represent your prospects then the ones above the line represent lost revenue and the ones below represent no sale. Either way XYZ is losing either profit or market share."

Dave asks, "How do we ever know?"

Barb says, "The very best practice is to let the customers pick[34] their own price. Given the opportunity we can see if that is possible."

---

[34]   A quick example of such a process is the "auction." Other examples are discussed and
      illustrated in the companion books.

"I'm confused," says Dave, "but let's investigate." (Refer to Appendix B.3)

Briefing Session

"This has been an experience but here is what it looks like. Because your offering is unique in each time period there is a set of people that want it to be fresh. They want it hot first thing because they feel the greatest benefit from being first. They are willing to pay a premium for freshness."

"Then there is another set that is not quite as anxious. A third set shop mostly average price and don't care about freshness and then finally there are the fire sale people."

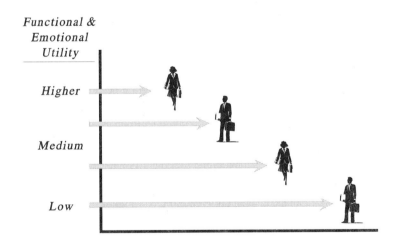

Decision Time

Variable Price

A more robust objective
can be realized. Consider
that if demand and price
are known, it is possible to
form a system that will
increase revenue with no
extra cost.

The price configuration recommended is a follows:

First 20 each day	$40/unit
Next 30 each day	$35/unit
Next 30 each day	$25/unit
Remainder each day	$20/unit

This table shows that the marketplace is willing to pay more for
items that are "hot off the press."

The maximum monthly revenue that the system generates when
96 units are produced per day and are sold according to the
price/demand relationship above is $87,600, compared to
$86,400 in the single price configuration. The profit for one
month using the variable pricing method is shown for the
original system configuration and for Configuration 2 below.
The pricing method suggested by the value engineer is put into
place and the profits again increase as expected.

		Maximum Revenue	Lost Revenue Due To Failures	System Cost	Monthly Profit
Reliability Impact	Base Configuration @ $30 Fixed Price	$86,400	$25,920	$12,000	$48,480
	Configuration 2 @ $30 Fixed Price	$86,400	$14,400	$20,000	$52,000
Price Impact	Base Configuration @ Tiered Price	$87,600	$26,280	$12,000	$49,320
	Configuration 2 @ Tiered Price	$87,600	$14,600	$20,000	$53,000

Dave schedules a bigger celebration party. This time he seeks out the information engineer. "Please come back again and explain exactly what happened in these improvements." (Refer to Appendices B.4, B.5)

Information Briefing

"What happened here was choices, refinement of choices and focus."

"When the system was established years ago choices were necessarily made as to how to form the processes. Here is what happened. The information which went into the process dictated that one component per stage be configured (Base Configuration). The reliability was destined by the **choices** made at that time."

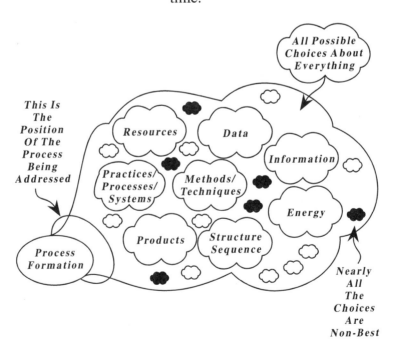

"If no data are collected about the success or failure rates of the components or if the data are selfishly biased by the group interests, then the return on most any choice of investment will likely be reduced. The information biases the solutions and, subsequently, the Return on Investment (ROI). The failure or success rate of the investment choices tend to be minimum investment rather than 'best' investment. Minimum is not best. Best is Best."

What the reliability engineer did was to "reopen" the book of choices and select a better business configuration from the set of choices. Information was the key ingredient. Information about the possibilities, about the nature of reliability, and information about the situation. She chose an ensemble that best fit the needs for the situation.

"Joe was a most interesting social case. He was required to make a choice also. He needed to choose between self interest, group interest and system interest. You, Dave, focused on the system interest and helped Joe see it also. You provided the balance."

"The very same choice thing happened in price setting. The choice XYZ made some time ago was unreliable. It was not backed by either information analysis or natural or social science. It was a guess. When you gave the opportunity to reopen the book of choices a better choice appeared."

"The degree of information present controlled the outcomes in all of these events. The ability of the team to cooperate was critical. Profit control is simply a matter of information control."

"Here is the numerical analysis of what happened."

Starting Profit $48,480

		Profit	Information
Reliability	to	$52,000/mo.	+5.36 units
Pricing	to	$53,000/mo	+3.50 units

"XYZ implemented higher information content through redundancy reliability into the business process. The teamwork of the duplicate components made the system smarter about performance."

"Next, XYZ implemented a higher information content, more knowledgeable market engagement and exchange system. The configuration was implemented through pricing."

"The combination of these two things began a path toward profit engineering through information engineering."

Dave says, "What next?" "The next step," says Barb, "is to locate the next highest variance of XYZ business consequence."

Case Summary — Points

In this case the reliability engineer performed information engineering as did the value engineer. The impact of the information "aggregated" and surfaced as XYZ profitability.

Each of the two (or more) processes that were reconfigured have a higher information content after than before.

8. CAPITALIZING

ON

INFORMATION DIFFERENTIALS

Information Wants to Be Free

Information exchange is particularly interesting. Consider that the buyer cannot know exactly what is missing else it would not be missing and therefore not be valuable. Consider that the supplier cannot know exactly what the buyer needs because the buyer does not know exactly. Consider that if the buyer discloses the magnitude of the uncertainty consequence, the price will be raised. Finally, consider that the buyer will not buy anything unseen. For the seller to explain it, the value drops to zero.

This is the *Nature of Information*.

Because the pricing process is purely an information process and because of the high emotion, it is a good candidate for illustration.

Pricing Information - Capturing the Fair Share of Worth

Pricing of information delivery is not different from any other object of worth except for the fragile characteristic of exclusivity.

Information contracting is delicate. The nature of information is such that the agreement must be made prior to disclosing the answer. If the buying party receives the "aha" information moment filling in the valuable missing ingredient, the exchange value disappears. On the other hand, the customer requires assurances of Return on Investment. This is a roadblock and barrier in the absence of rigorous metrics.

Throughout time the solution has been repackaging. Consultants sell their time but deliver information. Software is sold as a package but delivers information. Until just now information itself was not measurable.

A case can be made for expressing information services requirements in terms of uncertainty. If this were practiced the measures of cost and value would emerge very rapidly. For example, the requirement for invoice processing would be to minimize the uncertainty as to whether payment has been received. This is a trivial case but close. The greater, more valuable uncertainty lies beyond the invoice. The valuable uncertainty is how much customers value what?

All best practices in value based pricing and worth based pricing follow the same model for all objects (including information). The use is denied until the fee for use is agreed upon. An important previous diagram is repeated.

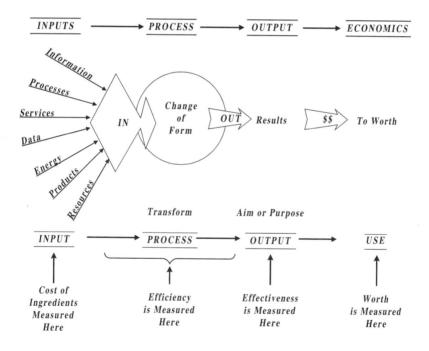

In the diagram substitute "pricing points" for "measuring points." In pricing to worth, the focus of the dialogue is the measurement and the moves to the right at least to effectiveness if not beyond. It is simple. If something genuinely magnifies positive results, price at the results point(s) is magnified also.

The return is far greater than pricing the ingredients. The sales adage is — "sell the product of the product." The price adage is "price to results." The return is guaranteed to be fair to **both** parties.

Nowhere is this more important than information delivery. The prerequisite is, of course, information value determination methodology.[35]

At What Price?

Commercial exchange transactions are bartered at an exchange price. Up trades, down trades and borrowing are permitted, but eventually everything in aggregate is balanced to zero. Such is the case with individual commercial exchanges.

Each side in a commercial exchange is contending for an advantageous price. The process in question on each side is the pricing process. One is sending price and the other is receiving price. Pricing process is one of the processes which is completely informational. The output of each party's process is an information object termed price.

Both parties can profit from the exchange transaction and usually do. Were this not the case, agreement would not occur. In any particular arbitration there is not necessarily a tight connection between the price and the energy required to create the offering being bartered. Only in the grand accumulation must the exchanges balance. The net profit or loss happens later down stream or up stream. The discontinuities cause ripples and waves of profit.

---

[35]   Refer to "Value Ledgers" and The Information Advantage.

Price is a critical, emotional, high consequence information element. As such it is a candidate for valuable information. In a blind (no previous price) arbitration both sides protect from disclosing their range of acceptable prices. Knowing the price of the other side would constitute valuable information (refer to the criteria). Knowing would provide an information based competitive advantage. The odds would shift to the holder of the information to maximize the exchange in their favor. What we have shown is the manner in which to calculate that advantage.

The negative consequence of "at cost" internal pricing can perhaps be seen. High worth items are exchanged at commodity fees. In the absence of (secondary) valuable information for determining profit points within the enterprise, all control is jeopardized. Neither the input, the output nor the difference is evident. Transfer pricing at cost implements a policy that says, "You can sell everything you make regardless of the inefficiency and/or the worth."

Luck vs. Information

Luck (probably) does happen. Chance events seem to occur. Valuable information behaves and "looks" much like luck. In fact, the operationalization of dynamic stochastic systems is implemented with the rule that says, "Give **good luck** the best chance to happen."

The difference between luck and information can be detected in the criteria for valuable information. Luck is not, for example, transportable, reproducible, controlling, reliable, etc. Information wears the disguise of luck. Sustained luck is information based. When the odds begin consistently favoring one side or the other, information is happening (refer to blackjack[36]). With a small percentage change (to 51 percent from say 49 percent) one could own Las Vegas.

---

[36]   The Information Advantage, op.cit., pp. 424-446.

The technique called "information mining" uses statistical inference engines to detect pattern anomalies in data that are different from normal. Attempts to explain the natural and unnatural "vectors" apparent in the data often yield information.

The Edge In Competitive Edge

Information monopolies occasionally exist (refer to Rothschild)[37] but more typically a competitive situation exists. Multiple suppliers contend for customer exchanges.

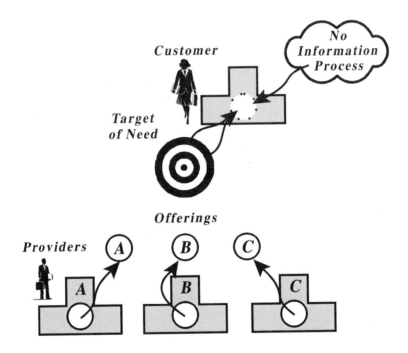

---

37   Ahead of Time, includes an information brief of the Rothschild scenario. For a more complete description see Morton, Frederic, 1962. The Rothschilds; A Family Portrait. New York: Curtis Company.

The contention for customer favor involves another set of choices. We call this the price-offering-worth process. Among other considerations the overall worth in the determination of the customer considers choices which have been made relating to functional utility, emotional utility, the channel of value delivery and the synergy of joint total worth. A very small information monopoly can leverage huge returns in the scenario. The difference of a few percentage points (odds) advantage in a large market is a significant edge. The issue here is similar to the lyrics of the Kenny Rogers song: "Know When to Hold'em, Know When to Fold'em and Know When to Walk Away." "Knowing" means being certain.

The pricing process is one of the fundamental core processes of the enterprise. It is rarely, if ever, engineered, noted, discussed, reengineered, taught or mentioned. There is an information VOID.

The resulting event of outcome is most likely to favor the provider firm which possesses the lower information entropy in the sum total of the processes. The information entropy is the sum of the products and consequences of the **choices**. Thus the measurement of the power, or edge, is determined by calculating the variance in the results among the participating entities.

9. EXTENDED APPLICATIONS

ROI and Return on Information — EV-IV

The previous two chapters generally have been about the
intersection of Economic Value (EV) and Information Value
(IV). Although there are multiple primitive measures of enterprise goodness, the most familiar is Return on Investment. We
will expand on it here because of its familiarity and, most of
all, because it follows the output over input metric form.

Tracking Towards Goals

From all we have learned about **Output/Input** and Variation and
Information and Control, consider that business Return on
Investment **(ROI = Output Return/Input Investment)** follows
the model described.

Now, if the goal is high **Output Return/Input Investment** and
choices from the candidate list (financial committee) are
chosen with high information content, then the observed ROI
will invariably track toward goal. Any variance will constitute
an information limitation shortcoming.

In this example, the performance results in the following ROI pattern over the interval 1990 - 1995:

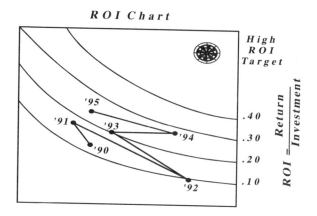

The enterprise demonstrates high variance toward its ROI goal reflecting statements about the information control typical when decisions are being made with insufficient information.

Here's another example:

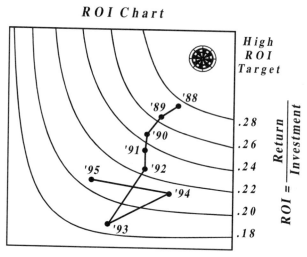

This is a case where information deficiencies are leading to decisions that distance the enterprise from its high ROI goal.

Finally, here is a case where valuable information is provoking steady progress toward goal.

R O I Chart

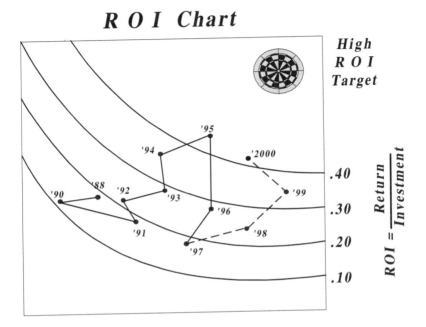

Notice the control aspects and the relationship to "vibes" presented earlier. If ROI is exhibiting "control," the track would necessarily adapt directly toward the goal. The existence of negative vibrations in ROI demonstrates the symptom of an information deficiency.

Note also that the overall methodology is often used for projection. It is not a requirement that the information be isolated in the past. Information may reference the future.

IV – Information Content Calculations

Consider that an enterprise exhibits the ROI characteristics as determined in the following time track diagram.

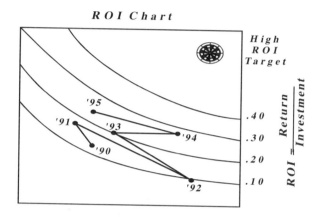

To show the information content relationship in connection with the "tracks" just discussed, we can illustrate the simplicity of the calculations.

The data to accomplish elementary tracks is not severe. Of course, more sophistication may require additional data. The data on the next page are sufficient for calculating the track above and several other varieties. The choice of whether to use assets or expenses for the horizontal axis is optional.

Moreover, the amount of informational value associated with the entity that exhibits the data can also be determined. All of these various computations are explained in Appendix A. The data on the next page are used multiple times to illustratae various insights.

The base enterprise data are shown in the following table.

	Revenue	Expenses	Net Profits	Assets	ROI (asset)
1990	115,970	110,172	5,798	49,140	0.118
1991	189,460	179,487	9,973	53,048	0.188
1992	99,975	94,576	5,399	53,719	0.101
1993	290,365	276,589	13,776	68,674	0.201
1994	540,792	515,252	25,540	90,566	0.282
1995	402,460	380,887	21,573	88,414	0.244

ROI is discussed in Appendix A as a decision system, control system and accounting system. The content analysis techniques and meanings are also discussed. The data shown here are used for the time track on the previous page and several in Appendix A. A point is made below relating to the last column of fractional ROI.

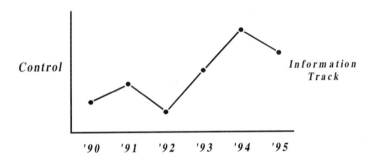

Note that the separation between the points on the graphic are different than one would expect from the numerical ROI data. The reason is that the vertical axis (although unscaled here) properly represents the amount of inherent control. In a sense, what happens is the amplification of the difference to the proper degree representing the valuable control content.

Return on Investment has the attribute of being a "proper" entropic metric. Because of the proper construction, the diagrams can be "mapped" to include both the economic (EV) and information (IV) content.

The diagram below shows both the information and the economic axes.

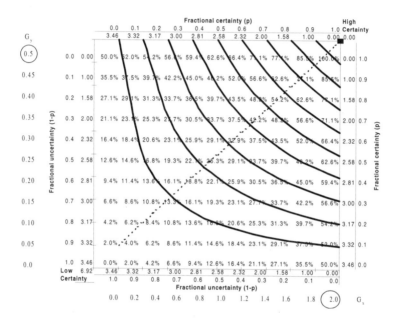

The following is a brief interpretation. A fuller explanation of this important concept can be found in Appendix A, page 240.

Vertical Axis. The economic value of Net Income divided by Revenue is the conventional calculation for half of the ROI equation. Along side the vertical axis is an uncertainty scale (u) and a certainty scale (c). These are the equivalent information metrics. As the certainty of achieving Net/Rev goes up and the uncertainty reduces, the probability of goal gain raises correspondingly.

Horizontal Axis. Revenue divided by Investment (assets) is the other half of the conventional ROI equation. As the certainty of controlling this metric raises, the goal achievement increases.

If the goal were to be established at say 30 percent ROI, then "certainty" or full information content knowledge would result in a 100 percent goal achievement.

Goal control would be assured. Any lesser goal achievement control is due to the amount of information deficiency (uncertainty) graphed in the diagram.

EV-IV diagrams work in this same manner for ALL properly formed measures and metrics. It is not always possible to separate the components into a two dimensional view. The two dimensional ROI diagram is possible because of the two multiplied terms that comprise the composite.

The latter half of Appendix A develops a complete description of the EV–IV relationship.

Industrial Case - Valuable Information Systems

One of the most remarkable properties of information content analysis is the incredibly high amount of content imbedded in a very small amount of unique data. This was symbolized at the beginning by the "squeezing of information secrets" out of regular old data. Another powerful example was offered concerning the Archer (page 111) requiring NO detailed efficiency data to measure effectiveness. The case of the "passenger" lost at sea involved a 50 percent content improvement from a **single word.**

Hence, it should not be surprising that the EV-IV control personality of an enterprise, its unique enterprise fingerprint, exists with very, very little data.

It should NOT be surprising based on what is written here:

- If ROI is not exhibiting proper directional control — the cause and corrective action is informational.

- If revenue is not exhibiting proper directional control — the cause and corrective action is informational.

- If goal gains are not exhibiting proper control — the cause and correction is informational.

- Back office and front office processes are information content intense.

ONE of several personality traits of an enterprise is Return on Investment. This signature is a telltale characteristic of the enterprise attitude toward business.

As it turns out this is one of the significant integrative metric signatures of every enterprise.

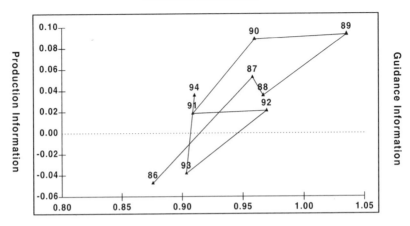

As few as a dozen composite measures and metrics define the competitive properties of an enterprise. Return on Investment is one. The next section depicts other strong candidates. Integrative metrics are composed of lower level primitives to form composites. The problem to date has been the uniform scaling of the metrics.

Enterprise Competitive Edges

Mastery of the techniques allows for the integrated development of a consistent measurement and display scale. Combinations of critical enterprise competitive characteristics can be
illustrated on the same basis (finally).

Characteristics which we recommend include the following list
and diagram at a minimum.

To illustrate how this works consider an example of 32 enterprises in the energy industry.

A "certainty" diagram is constructed with each spoke representing an equal scale of certainty. Because of the extended
measurement capabilities, it is possible to quantify very important enterprise characteristics.

On a single enterprise basis, Lyondell (one of the thirty-two participants) has been selected for display.

LYONDELL PETROCHEMICAL CO

These measures track the characteristics mentioned. "Balance" means profitability (the balance between revenue and cost).

Significant others can be added to exactly the same diagram. In this case the entries are a portion of industry competitors. In fact, the top quartile (eight of the thirty-two) are shown.

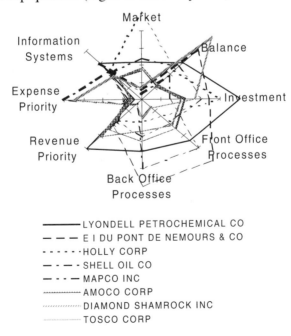

LYONDELL PETROCHEMICAL CO
E I DU PONT DE NEMOURS & CO
HOLLY CORP
SHELL OIL CO
MAPCO INC
AMOCO CORP
DIAMOND SHAMROCK INC
TOSCO CORP

For those readers interested in knowledge engineering or information engineering and perhaps those interested in cognition, we will show on the same scale the fourth (bottom) quartile set of enterprises.

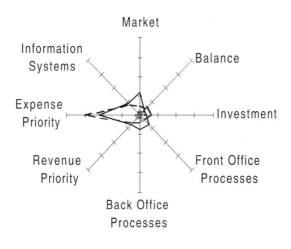

─────── CLARK R&M HOLDINGS INC
─ ─ ─ ─ SUN CO INC
· · · · · · · CROWN CENTRAL PETROLEUM CORP
─ · ─ · ─ WAINOCO OIL CORP
─ · · ─ · LOUISIANA LAND & EXPLORATION CO
∼∼∼∼∼∼ TESORO PETROLEUM CORP
∼∼∼∼∼∼ TRANSAMERICAN REFINING CORP
············· ARABIAN SHIELD DEVELOPMENT CO

The reader notices that the scale is too small to see. This is because their information content (knowledge) is very low relative to those previously shown. If we amplify this scale then we must magnify the previous first quartile also.

Learning is a rate of change metric. In our view organizational learning is the rate of change of valuable information content. One can now see the absolute prerequisite to be able to calculate valuable information content in order to determine the rate of change of it for "learning" measurements. Having satisfied that prerequisite for this group of enterprises, we can show in list form the dynamics or organizational learning directed at the topic of investment.

Return On Investment Learning											
ID	Name	94	93	92	91	90	89	88	87	86	85
LYO	LYONDELL PETROCHEMICAL CO	1	25	12	1	1	1	1	1		
HOC	HOLLY CORP	2	1	18	4	2	2	2	19	1	6
DD	E I DU PONT DE NEMOURS & CO	3	22	6	6	8	3	6	2	2	2
AN	AMOCO CORP	4	4	10	7	9	6	8	4	8	1
CHV	CHEVRON CORP	5	7	1	9	4	18	11	6	11	3
DRM	DIAMOND SHAMROCK INC	6	15	11	11	10	5	9			
P	PHILLIPS PETROLEUM CO	7	12	7	13	11	17	10	20	9	5
TOS	TOSCO CORP	8	3	4	5	3	20	3	5	20	18
MUR	MURPHY OIL CORP	9	9	9	18	5	7	16	23	23	4
FI	FINA INC	10	17	16	17	15					
CECX	CASTLE ENERGY CORP	11	10	31	29	24	19	4	3	6	24
D.PKB	PDV AMERICA INC	12	11	5	8						
ARSD	ARABIAN SHIELD DEVELOPMENT CO	13	30	27	20	27	25	26	24	15	20
MDA	MAPCO INC	14	2	2	2	7	4	7	8	5	8
ULR	ULTRAMAR CORP	15	5	15	12	26					
TSO	TESORO PETROLEUM CORP	16	14	29	21	17	26	23	22	24	23
D.ACR	ASHLAND OIL INC	17	18	26	14	18	21	14	9	4	14
KMG	KERR MCGEE CORP	18	21	22	10	22	12	15	12	22	10
UCL	UNOCAL CORP	19	8	8	16	19	13	21	17	13	12
CGP	COASTAL CORP	20	23	23	24	21	22	18	16	14	16
AHC	AMERADA HESS CORP	21	29	14	19	14	8	19	10	17	17
GI	GIANT INDUSTRIES INC	22	19	24	27	23	9	12			
SUN	SUN CO INC	23	6	28	26	20	23	22	11	12	11
VLO	VALERO ENERGY CORP	24	16	3	3	6	16	17	18	19	15
D.SGU	SHELL OIL CO	25	20	13	23	16	10	13	7	10	7
WOL	WAINOCO OIL CORP	26	26	21	28	28	24	20	13	21	22
CNPA	CROWN CENTRAL PETROLEUM CORP	27	27	25		12	15	5	25	18	21
D.TMB	TRANSAMERICAN REFINING CORP	28	31	30							
PZL	PENNZOIL CO	29	13	19	22	25	11	24	14	7	9
LLX	LOUISIANA LAND & EXPLORATION CO	30	24	20	15	13	14	25	15	16	19
CRM	CLARK R&M HOLDINGS INC			28	17						
PRI	PACIFIC RESOURCES, INC.								21	3	13

The reader can perhaps see the extensions to this path. If customers and prospects were populated on the list instead of competitors, the technique would yield a powerful sales and marketing tool. If merger or acquisition candidates were used as the population, then it is much easier to "see" synergies and patterns of "fit."

The book Ahead of Time extends this chain substantially. A theme named "ITOP"—Information Technique for Optimizing Performance, Productivity and Profit—is developed utilizing these measures, techniques and approaches. To the extent of your interest in the extensions please refer to that work.

10. CONCLUSION

GIVE GOOD LUCK
THE BEST ODDS OF HAPPENING.

Summary and Conclusion

If one takes a pack of cards as it comes from the manufacturer and shuffles it for a few minutes, the original order disappears. **Something** has been done to scramble the **orderly** arrangement of this 52 element set.

Nature's laws fall into two groups. First, we can study those laws that control the behavior of a single object. Clearly, no shuffling can occur in these problems—it does not make sense to separate the King of Spades and shuffle him by himself. Secondly, we can study the processes of nature in **groups** of objects. Our treatment here much relates to the problem of the pack, not of the isolated card.

The cards can be put back into their original order by sorting. Note, however, that ordering takes a certain **rationality** beyond that of shuffling. Shuffling can be accomplished absentmind-edly, ordering cannot. Thus, order and information are con-nected. Ordering implies identity on the cards of their rank. Reordering blank, faceless or invisible cards is not possible. The guarantee of the reorder being achieved depends on the ability to identify and MEASURE the degree of ORGANIZA-TION.

To accomplish our aim we have had to raise "organization" from a vague descriptive term to one of the measurable quanti-ties of exact science. We are confronted by many kinds of organizations and the lack of them. The uniform march of the band is not the only form of organized motion; the members of a stage chorus organize their sound waves to create harmony. A common measure can be applied to all forms of organization. Any loss of organization is equitably measured by the chance against its recovery by an accidental coincidence (luck). The chance is often regarded as contingency, but it is **precise** as a **measure**.

To make certain that the measure links to familiar science we use the energy laws. We consider things like falling stones, not for their energy component but for their organizational component.

As the stone falls it inherits an attribute of kinetic energy, the amount of which would be just right to lift it back to the original height. When the stone contacts a surface, its kinetic energy is connected to heat-energy. There is still the same total quantity, if we could scrape it together and **reorganize** it back together (like Humpty-Dumpty).

Looking deep inside the falling stone we see an enormous multitude of molecules moving downward with equal and parallel velocities. This is a form of the organized motion, like the band marching down the field.

Two separate things can be seen, the energy and the **organization** of the energy. To return Humpty-Dumpty or the stone to the original position, **BOTH** energy and **organization** of the energy must be restored.

To restore the stone (and to sort the cards) we must supply extraneous energy which has the required amount of organization. The secret of information (or lack of it) is held in the energy organization component. It is what we call the amount of information content.

Information, like energy, is not particularly valuable unless it can be harnessed and directed to utility. Processes do exactly that because process is also, exactly and only an energy with its informational component controlling the orderly sorting of sequence.

People conduct business and place value on objects and items. Physical science refuses to address people thinking and the idea of thought. People sciences do that. Just before leaving physical science an apparent discontinuity is created because of the two types of laws (single object and multiple group). People get confused.

Some events never happen in the physical world because they are impossible, others because they are too improbable. The role and responsibility of the single object laws are to define the first part, the impossibilities. People cannot fly unaided or break the laws of gravity. These are called deterministic. The laws which forbid the second address group probabilities and organization (the information part).

Many times the answers to an important question apparently conflict. For example, can time go backward? Primary law answers, "Yes, it is not impossible." The second set answers, "No, it is too improbable." The result is both a "yes" and "no" from the sciences. Can ten thousand packs of cards be shuffled back to order by random shuffling?

Yes, No.

Both answers are true depending on the choice of laws.

The context of value is brought in by people and groups of people called enterprises conducting trade with high emotional and financial consequence.

When probability of goal gain is based on the limitation of information (and it most often is), then every meaningful information piece alters (personalizes) the probability of event particulars. It makes no difference, in the probability sense, whether the event is past or future. The past event of which a person possesses no certain information is as much a subject of probability as the future possible event.

The observation of any part of the event (or none of it) is simply a knowledge gain with respect to the event in either case. As a consequence, the VERY SAME event will be UNEQUALLY probable to different people whose previous NEWS will have differed by a bit or a much greater amount.

In the introduction essay (page 16) someone, perhaps the friend, was lost at sea. The first message said only that, and the odds were thirty-five to one. (This is the uniform natural basis). The second message said it was a passenger. Whomever received that message now holds better odds at five to one. (This is the content difference.) If one person receives the message and the other does not, a substantial difference exists. The amount of information content difference is 50 percent. If this were not a tragic event but rather a business event of consequence, the difference in information greatly favors the holder of the latter news message versus only the former.

What is different between a past event (as above) and a future event is the exclusivity. Rareness with knowing the future is more assured. A future event is rationalized to be more fair and honest because the access to future is impossible and denied both parties. But, is it really?

If, however, the event is a repetition and/or if one observer has otherwise viewed a past event which happens to arise again (been there, done that), then the information or part of it may be available ahead of time. Education, training, practice or just regular experience all create possibilities of preparing to recognize future events and making better informed choices.

Whether between individuals or groups or enterprises, the relative certainty of one group versus the different uncertainty of the second group creates a potential information arbitrage which favors the holder of the best information particular to the consequential topic. The magnitude potential of the arbitrage is the difference in the respective probabilities times the consequence magnitude under consideration.

Information and particularly valuable information is a most precious asset. The wealth generating capacity of truly valuable information is greater than gold.

Mostly "news" is the same thing happening over and over again to different people. Sometimes, however, there are exceptions. This is what it is all about.

APPENDIX A

CALCULATING INFORMATION VALUE

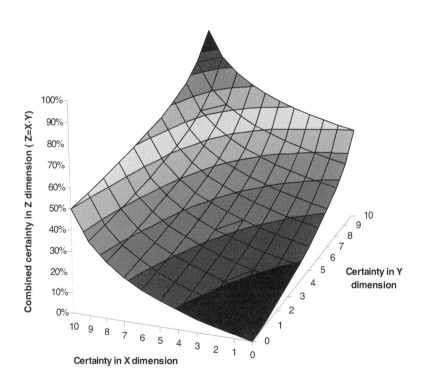

A.1   Measurement Processes and Systems Criteria

The process of measurement is itself wholly an informational process. The reader may well appreciate the extent to which huge amounts of data are generated from various aspects of measurements and the resulting interpretations of the measurement. The treatment here is brief. The aim is to position the measurement system described here among others commonly used.

The Measurement and Scaling Process

The typical goal of measurement processes is the assignment of quanta (numbers) to represent the magnitude of interesting or significant characteristic ingredients. Most often the numerical assignment goal is the proportional representation of the numbers to the property of interest.

One should suspect as a consequence of the goal that numbers, arithmetic and mathematics are likely to result. While quantification is the goal here, the general basis for all measurement is comparison. Measurement always constructs special kinds of difference comparisons. Comparison precedes measurement.

Degree and Kind

The differences measured by all information measuring processes are of two kinds. They are called differences in degree and differences in kind.

Quantity of an object is the kind of property that inherits or exhibits magnitude (degree). This property is contrasted with those objects that inherit or exhibit an all or none condition (for example, pregnancy).

Because the originating condition is based on differences, the notion of "relative" enters. Although it took thousands of years, it is generally agreed that we cannot speak of velocity of an object without at least an implicit reference to other objects. Velocity has come to be regarded as an essentially relative concept.

In our treatment herein we rely intimately upon the basis of relative difference comparisons. It is fundamental. So is it to **all other** measuring processes.

Measurement Groupings

Measurement information arises from two groups: fundamental and indirect. Fundamental measuring processes construct measures of primitives. Mass, time-interval and length are fundamental measures. The common trait is that they do not depend on anything else.

The diagram of groups is shown below.

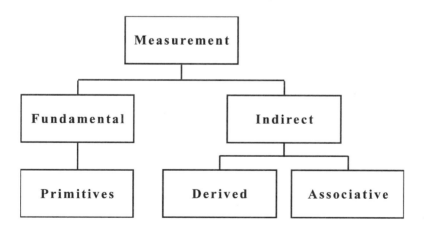

An indirect measure can be either derived or associative. Volume is a derived measure because if one can measure length then area and volume can be derived. Associative measures require the determination of a "correspondence principle." The choice of the correspondence relates to the functional relationship between one measure (length) and the other object properties (area, volume). Information content is a fundamental and primitive measure. Value is an association measure. The intersection is a hybrid. The information part is more technically rigorous than the value part.

Operationalization Procedures

As we have previously described in chapter 4, all processes are operationalized with rules. The rules associated with operationalizing proper measurement systems follow:

(a)   Measurement is the assignment of numbers to objects or events according to rule.

(b)   We have a measurement system if and only if we have a rule for assignment.

(c)   The rule shall be determinative in the sense that (given proper care) the same numbers or ranges would always be assigned to the same things under the same conditions.

(d)   The rule should be non-degenerative in the sense that it assigns different numbers to different things.

Scales and Models - Species

There are at least four species of scales that have served the needs for all measurement.

These four scales are:

> Nominal
> Ordinal
> Linear Interval
> Ratio

We call them species because there is an indefinite number of procedures in each scale which are implemented for the conduct of assignment. Several other subspecies arise from time to time as candidates. These are:

> Nominal — Interval
> Ordinal — Interval
> Log

These scales are a matter of convenience and can usually be considered a special case of the original four.

Examples:

> Nominal -   Sports team players are assigned a numeric identity under the rule that no two can be assigned the same number.

Ordinal -	"Hardness" is assigned a numerical value (Mohs) according to the arranged hardness of an object. The objects are arranged in order of ever-increasing hardness (monotonic) and assigned an appropriate proportional numerical value. The test of this scale is the fact that the harder object will scratch the less hard upon contact (but not the reverse). A diamond on glass is an example.
Linear Interval -	Temperature is a measure where each degree is proportional to more or less hot or cold.
Ratio -	Efficiency or effectiveness is measured in terms of the ratio of the differences in exchange processes.

Although independence in definition can be achieved, these scaling systems overlap one another in common use. The choice of scale is a matter of goal and often convenience.

Models

Mathematical models are used to convert observations into numerical measurements. The model is chosen to express intentions and not merely to describe the data.

Models are selected on the basis of attempting to state truthful predictions about current and future observations of the same condition without seriously introducing error. Two types of models exist which describe the rules under which the transformation from observations to quantification occurs and which limit the statements concerning the results.

Deterministic - Deterministic models imply exact and certain predictability of outcomes. This can be accomplished when there is certainty that all causes have been included and the precise transformations are known. Small errors are present but ignored because the values of interest trivialize the error.

Stochastic, Probabilistic - When the make up of outcome causing variables is unknown or impractically large or when similar circumstances create a variety of outcomes, statistical models are used. As in the deterministic case the statistical model attempts to state exactly **what is known** and **what is unknown** in a measured scale.

Comprehensive, Integrated - Information and value each span both deterministic and stochastic. Accomplishing complete information valuation measure must be sufficiently robust to be comprehensive.

Units

Units must retain the same meaning throughout the operating range of the scale of the variables. Sameness of scale is, therefore, a necessary and sufficient condition for sameness of units.

Calculating Information Value - The Measurement System

In the measuring and scaling of information what we have
described is the linkage between variation, information, energy
dissipation and economics. Certain information is much more
valuable than other information. It follows that certain variation measures are much more valuable to control enterprise
destiny than others. This schematic highlights the topics in the
enterprise that will yield the greatest returns for the energy
invested.

Total Cost Curve For Optimizing Freedom And Control

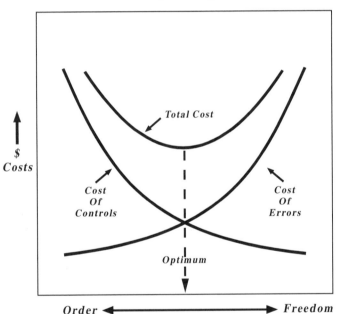

This classic optimization diagram appears in several disciplines. In economics it is referenced as the "Laffer curve"
relating government revenue to rate of taxation. It appears in
atomic physics referencing the binding energy and atomic
weight relationship. In psychology it is shown as the productivity and stress curve.

The relationship described here is similar. Control is **only** achieved by information. The cost of control is the cost of information to exercise the degree of control appropriate. Moreover, the cost of error is merely the consequence of lack of information. "Certainty" can be substituted for the curve labeled "cost of control." "Cost of uncertainty" can be substituted for the "error" curve.

Next we will restate the vocabulary slightly. We suggest that it is not appropriate that the singular goal of business enterprise is to minimize cost. While necessary, it is not a sufficient condition. A more beneficial objective would seem to be the maximization of worth. This alteration is a substantial information difference.

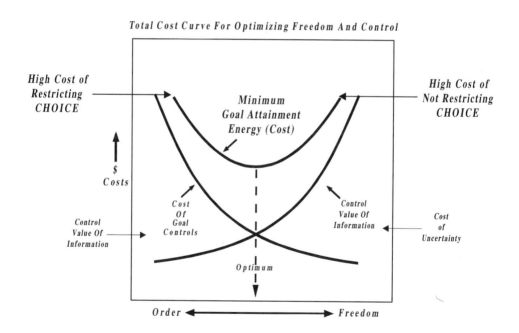

Total Cost Curve For Optimizing Freedom And Control

Value and Valuation

The metric for information content can be determined independent of value as shown in several of the examples (Red Ball, Archer and Reliability). The joining of "value" imposes additional considerations. Objects acquire value attributes in relation to the degree in which they satisfy or potentially <u>satisfy recipient goal attainment</u> velocity or acceleration. Notice that a sufficient goal condition may be the negative avoidance or anti-consequence case. <u>Avoidance of the worst is a valid and measurable goal condition.</u>

For example, if the goal is cost reduction, an object is valuable to the measure and extent that it is able to reduce costly errors during use. If the goal is revenue, the object is valuable when it accomplishes revenue acceleration. As a consequence units of value are obligated to take on the units of recipient goal.

It Follows

To the extent the goal is absent or unknown, so are the valuation units. Remember the anti-consequence goal.

To the extent that the goal measures are subjective, so are the valuation measures.

To the extent that the goal measures are quantifiable, so are the valuation measures.

Considerable discussion in the text has been devoted to groups and teams. The reader may conclude that somehow this technique is dependent on groups. This is not the case. The group discussion particularly relates to goals and goal definition (refer to Joe in the reliability example). Information is important to the goal of the receiver — whatever the real goal turns out to be. The authors have found it necessary in some cases to build tools that surface, isolate and solidify goals.

A-10

The information content measure is uncaring about the worth of the goal. Only goal attainment matters. It is the value measure which is economic and/or emotional caring.

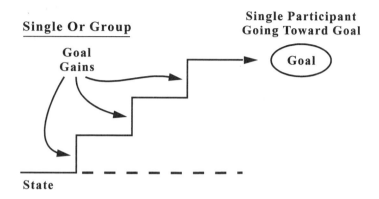

The measuring technique works equally well whether there are one or more participants (refer to archer). As with all measures the outcome differs with the design intention. The difference is rather like process improvement versus process benchmarking. The most typical case for information content measure is the comparative measure of one entity's content versus that of significant others. An example would measure one enterprise versus its competitors, customers and suppliers.

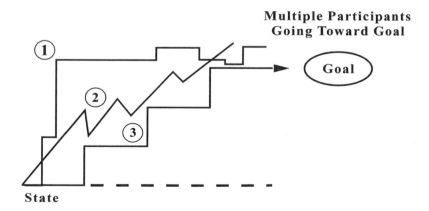

In cases where multiple participants seek the same goal, comparative measures can also be accomplished.

Monetization Techniques

The manner in which financial analyses are applied is conventional. The differences, if any, are in the time period of consideration (past or future) and the use of receiver economic situation as the basis for computations. The techniques are shown below and are well treated in other relevant literature.

Technique	*Measure*
Replacement ● *In Kind* ● *With Future In Mind*	● *Substitution Difference In Use*
Rate ● *Success — Acceleration* ● *Failure — Avoidance*	● *Quantity Differences* ● *Achievement Rate Difference*
● *Market — Growth*	● *Revenue Difference*
● *Relative To Others*	● *Difference Relative To Others*
● *Composite*	● *All Of Above Differences*

A more rigorous treatment of valuation method and technique exists in the field of utility theory. von Neumann and Morgenstern[40], for example, develop an axiomatic approach guaranteeing cardinal (numeric scaled) utility functions. Their methods involve decision preference attitudes toward various uncertain outcomes.

---

[40]   Theory of Games and Economic Behavior, John von Neumann and Oskar Morgenstern, Princeton University Press, Princeton, N.J., 1947.

A.2   The JT JB Information Content Measuring System

History

The statistical foundation of our measure was begun by
Abraham De Moivre back in the 18th century. The work
unified the Bernoulli trial and resulted in the binomial distribution, plus combinatorial mathematics. The Pascal Triangle and
the binomial coefficients form the normal distribution linkage.
The grand result was the creation of the Central Limit Theorem.

Recall that the binomial distribution occurs when there are just
two possible outcomes, pass-fail, heads-tails, win-lose, etc.
One of the outcomes is a success and the other failure. The
Bernoulli trial has three critical properties.

1.   The result of each trial is either a success or failure.
2.   The probability "**p**" of success is the same in every trial.
3.   The trials are <u>independent</u> in that the outcome of one
      trial has no influence on later outcomes.

An important feature of our measure unfolds when the outcome
of one trial <u>has</u> influence over the next because this is the
evidence that **information content** has changed. Refer to
property 3 above in regard to Bayes' comments on page A-17.

De Moivre showed that when **p** = .5 the binomial yielded a
continuous density function called the "normal" distribution.
The standardized normal works the same for any value of "**p**".
In effect, all binomials turn into normals eventually when the
number of trials "**n**" gets large.

The more general result shows why the normal is so prevalent
in nature. Data that are influenced by many small **random**
situational interactions are normally distributed. Stock market

fluctuations, height, weight, yearly temperature averages and S.A.T. scores are results of many different informational effects but all tend toward normal.

The Central Limit Theorem states that if one measures a situation "**n**" times that has a mean of μ and standard deviation σ, then as **n** gets large, the distribution of estimates of mean μ approaches the normal distribution with standard deviation σ/n. The remarkable feature is that regardless of the original distribution, the taking of averages guarantees a normal.

Please note the conformance along the path with the context of information and information entropy.

The Method

> ### Valuation of Information
>
> The simple measure of information worth is the product of the goal oriented certainty content (if any) beyond natural **times** the goal reward consequence **plus** the product of the remaining goal UNcertainty content (if any) **times** the natural equilibrium reward
> — relative to —
> natural equilibrium consequence alone.

Information is proven to be the only controlling entity. Therefore, the amount of lack of control is proportional to the lack of information certainty (uncertainty). Hence, we precisely measure that amount of natural uncontrol versus actual uncontrol and associate the difference with the reward for greater control.

The method is simple. Determine the underlying "natural" entropy distribution for the case (whatever the distribution really is). Calculate the various natural and man-made control measures including variance and entropy (steps 1 through 4 below).

A-14

Next use the observation data measured from the actual encounters with the system (step 5). Compare the results.

Consideration is given as to whether best, worst or average information content is the interpretation. The information content computation can be accomplished independently of or in conjunction with value. Value is associated with the content measure in proportion to the degree of the total worth control.

Calculation Steps

The design and calculation activities for information content are:

1.   Define the boundaries of the process or system for which the information content is to be measured.

2.   Decide whether the objective of the measure includes measuring the aiming information content, the construction information content or both.

3.   Construct the measurement metric which is equivalent to the situation. Give consideration to the observation data which will be subsequently matched to determine the continuous or discrete form of the natural.

    Helpful Notes:

    •   At least one and often three conditions will always be known. The minimum information condition and distribution; the maximum information condition and distribution; and/or the average information condition and distribution.   Any one of the three forms a necessary and sufficient calculation basis.

- ᴼᵘᵗᵖᵘᵗ/ᴵₙₚᵤₜ relative to aiming or production is a good starting point.

- Uniform in the case of discrete and normal in the case of continuous are first search likelihoods.

4. Given the measuring situation and design, calculate the equivalent **natural** system result. Determine mean, standard deviation and most important of all the entropy.

5. Take measurements of the **actual** sample case. Determine mean, standard deviation and most important of all the entropy.

6. Compare the actual statistical result (step 5) with the base case (step 4).

7. The information content in the process being measured is the difference or comparison that results from step 6.

8. The monetization step is either direct or indirect. If the design metric constructed in step 3 is already to a financial scale (monetized) then the result will be the in economic (value) terms. If the design metric is in consequence terms other than financial (such as reliability) then another step will be required at a minimum and possibly another linked or associated measurement set. Such an activity set would be designed in the same fashion except with the added requirement in step 3 that the metric be economic value compatible.

Comments

There are notable differences in this method from "typical" statistical method.

First, there is no doubt as to the underlying distribution. By design, the metric distribution is KNOWN. Often it is normally distributed (or uniform). The content estimate of the information is the degree in which the observed differs from normal.

Second, we are measuring stochastic process entropy more closely resembling reliability engineering than typical population statistics. Conjecture is minimized by operating strictly within the intersecting constraints of previously proven natural laws. The error, if any, is in the ambiguous terminology (words) required to describe the phenomena and the laws themselves. This too is a recursive characteristic of information entropy. The path yields incredible fundamental essence, including the meaning of patterns, the origins of probabilities and life forms.

Third, as opposed to eliminating bias, the objective is to exactly target measuring the bias (without adding any additional). The amount of bias is the amount of information.

Information Relevance, Independence and Bayes' Equation

Information events being relevant to knowledge events introduce a certain intuitive connotation concerning the influencing of one event by another event. The degree of influencing interactions is treated in both probability and statistics (Bayes' Equation) and information theory. Here we will attempt to show the similarities and distinctions.

The treatment we shall pursue is illustrated in the following stages.

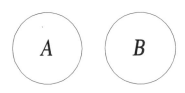

When two events (objects) are independent one to the other when there is no influence. 100% independent 0% dependent.

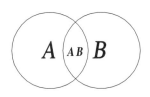

When two events are partially dependent one on the other there is a fractional gain in information relevance associated with one carrying over to the other.

When two events enclave or overlap, the information content on one is wholly the other but not the reverse.

When two events are identical, the information content is equivalent, equal and identical. They are one and the same. A semantic **DUALITY** exists.

Now let us more specifically redescribe the series and make verbal, probability and information theory statements.

Independence

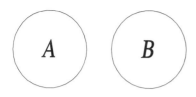

If two events are independent then there exists no relevant interaction including information interaction between the pair.

The chance of two independent events both happening is the product of their chance separately. One's chance has no influence on the other.

That is, $P(AB) = P(A) \cdot P(B)$.

And $P(B \mid A) = P(B)$ i.e., the probability of event B given event A is the same as the probability of event B. That is, the information about A does not provide information about B. So that

$$\frac{P(B \mid A)}{P(B)} = 1$$

and the information content $-p \log p$ is 0 since

$$\log \frac{P(B \mid A)}{P(B)} = \log 1 = 0.$$

Partial Dependence, Partial Independence

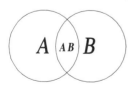

If two events are (information) dependent (not independent) then the information of either of the pair partially describes the other.

If the two events are not independent the chance that they should both happen is the product of the chance that the first should happen and the chance that when the first has happened the second should happen also.

AB is the partial amount of information relevant to both A and B.

Given A, an amount log $\dfrac{P\ (B\ |\ A)}{P\ (B)}$ of information about B is gained.

That is, P (B | A) ≥ P (B) and
     if P (B | A) = P (B)
       then B and A are independent

and log $\dfrac{P\ (B\ |\ A)}{P\ (B)}$ = log 1 = 0

and knowledge of A gives no information about B.

Given B, an amount log of $\dfrac{P\ (A\ |\ B)}{P\ (A)}$ information about A is gained.

That is, P (A | B) ≥ P (A) and
     if P (A | B) = P (A)
       then A and B are independent

and log $\dfrac{P\ (A\ |\ B)}{P\ (A)}$ = log 1 = 0

and knowledge of B gives no information about A.

Enclave or Overlap

The information content of AB is the complete information about A contained within a part of the whole B.

That is, A → B or A is a subset of B or A implies B.

Then P (B | A) = 1.
That is, given A, B is a certainty.

A-20

$$P(A \mid B) = P(A) \ \frac{P(B \mid A)}{P(B)} \quad \text{since } P(B \mid A) = 1 \text{ then}$$

$$P(A \mid B) = P(A) \ \frac{1}{P(B)}$$

i.e., given B, the amount $\log \dfrac{1}{P(B)}$ of information about A is gained.

$$\log \frac{1}{P(B)} = -\log P(B)$$

$$P(A) \le P(B) \le 1$$

Complete Interdependence—Duality

The smaller P (B) is the more information it carries about A. B carries maximum information regarding A when P (B) is smallest or P (B) ≡ P (A) then A becomes a certainty when B is true and the regions A and B coincide.

The point of all this is to note that the commonality in form and format between the Bayes' probability and the information theory. The difference is the logarithmic treatment consistently applied in information formulation and consistently not in probability. At the end of this appendix are profound implications of appreciating this last case. (See the **duality** discussion in *Methodology Review* and *Tracker Diagram (EV-IV and More)* on pages 257 and 258.) Most do not analyze or persist to this case. Semantic contamination is important here.

Torturous Trust and Validation

A serious mental difficulty arises relative to the concept of a "standard." Standards arise when we humans cooperatively decide that something must be commonized. The examples here are time and temperature. None of the necessary and sufficient measurement theory criteria requires that a measure be "standardized."

This particular information scaling technique is made difficult because of its <u>freedom</u> to be personal or group particular. A thing is **not less true** because it is not standardized and widely UNIFORM. This method does not follow the Rule of One (answer).

Rather it follows Rule of One method that yields correct but not uniform answers. In all likelihood there will not evolve a single uniform widely accepted information measurement scale. Rather there will be many equally correct scales. If you accept and practice this method, then **you** will possess a rather personal or group scale that you can use. When this happens it will appear to be a SECRET. Nonstandardized, true, unique, rare, personalized information appears to **others** as secrets. The encounter is one with regular old **valuable** information.

When you learned that $1 + 1 = 2$ you did so by receiving repetitive news about the match from **trusted** sources. Validation happened as much as any other reason because of the collective decision to standardize and make uniform that decision. Other alternatives, equally correct were and are available. $1 + 1 = 10$ in the base 2 numbering system is an example of an equally valid alternative.

This scale is every bit as correct and truthful. It is just different. Your choice of when you feel hot or cold is not dependent on Fahrenheit, Centigrade or Kelvin.

However, you choose one (or the other or all) to communicate the degree of hotness and coldness. More particularly you use these measures to **control** the temperature of your environment.

Simple Computational Techniques

We thought it appropriate to demonstrate the rigorous background to the topic. At the outset we mentioned that this may do more harm than good. Now we will show the simple techniques that permit wide application with a minimum of sophisticated mathematics.

The Ordered List Method

The simplest method for a group of objects is the ordered list. The reliability example used this form wherein each configuration represented an object line item in the list. The discrete entropy formula is appropriate.

- Choose any convenient log base (e.g., base 2).
- Select N items of group interest.
- The maximum entropy for a relative scale will be log N.

The information base 2 scale shown on page 103 is repeated here. This will be the relative information scale.

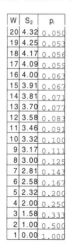

W	S₂	pᵢ
20	4.32	0.050
19	4.25	0.053
18	4.17	0.056
17	4.09	0.059
16	4.00	0.063
15	3.91	0.067
14	3.81	0.071
13	3.70	0.077
12	3.58	0.083
11	3.46	0.091
10	3.32	0.100
9	3.17	0.111
8	3.00	0.125
7	2.81	0.143
6	2.58	0.167
5	2.32	0.200
4	2.00	0.250
3	1.58	0.333
2	1.00	0.500
1	0.00	1.000

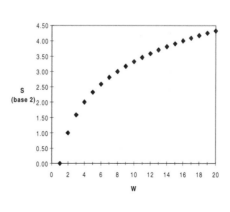

- Choose a meaningful ordering metric (the goal statistic). (Whatever "best" means.)
- Order the list of N objects from best to worst on the basis of the goal ordering statistic.
- Match the best with entropy equal zero and the worst with maximum entropy.

Example:

Measure the information content of a group of 20 industrial companies relative to the goal gain ordering metric of revenue divided by expense. Create a table or plot by matching the position on the ordered list to the corresponding entropy table ordinal entry (match line items).

Table or Plot the information content scale results.

The ordering statistic is represented by $D = R/E - 1$.
The following table comprises the raw data for the example:

Name	R($M)	E ($M)	D	SYM
Company A	8,963	8,767	.022	A
Company B	24,449	21,919	.115	B
Company C	34,703	31,835	.090	C
Company D	3,107	3,027	.027	D
Company E	34,743	31,542	.101	E
Company F	8,692	8,498	.023	F
Company G	442	415	.064	G
Company H	10,839	10,585	.024	H
Company I	4,595	4,250	.081	I
Company J	2,320	2,166	.071	J
Company K	9,005	8,773	.026	K
Company L	8,692	8,498	.023	L
Company M	2,131	2,062	.034	M
Company N	1,336	1,282	.042	N
Company O	1,650	1,564	.055	O
Company P	2,400	2,318	.035	P
Company Q	5,780	5,605	.031	Q
Company R	1,042	1,011	.030	R
Company S	2,335	2,261	.033	S
Company T	9,751	9,371	.041	T

Our results are shown below.

Rnk	Name	R ($M)	E ($M)	S	D	SYM
	Ordered by descending D					
1	Company B	24,449	21,919	0.00	.115	B
2	Company E	34,743	31,542	1.00	.101	E
3	Company C	34,703	31,835	1.58	.090	C
4	Company I	4,595	4,250	2.00	.081	I
5	Company J	2,320	2,166	2.32	.071	J
	Group	6,408	6,004		.067	
6	Company G	442	415	2.58	.064	G
7	Company O	1,650	1,564	2.81	.055	O
8	Company N	1,336	1,282	3.00	.042	N
9	Company T	9,751	9,371	3.17	.041	T
10	Company P	2,400	2,318	3.32	.035	P
11	Company M	2,131	2,062	3.46	.034	M
12	Company S	2,335	2,261	3.58	.033	S
13	Company Q	5,780	5,605	3.70	.031	Q
14	Company R	1,042	1,011	3.81	.030	R
15	Company D	3,107	3,027	3.91	.027	D
16	Company K	9,005	8,773	4.00	.026	K
17	Company H	10,839	10,585	4.09	.024	H
18	Company F	8,692	8,498	4.17	.023	F
19	Company L	8,692	8,498	4.25	.023	L
20	Company A	8,963	8,767	4.32	.022	A

Note that there was NO computation AT ALL in this process. The only thing that was necessary was the ORDERING of the raw data list. After the ordering, the twenty "S" numbers from the entropy scale were transferred to the resulting twenty ordered entries.

The plot of the information scale of goodness is shown as follows:

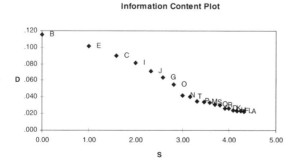

This plot now defines the complete range of the scale and the incremental information units.

The Distribution Match Method

The distribution match method is the least used in our experience because it requires the most assumptions and the most data. We have shown it for the insight as to what is happening.

The use of continuous distributions requires that real time dynamic data be available from the distribution. Parallel processing is then invoked to calculate the ebb and flow. Such a thing requires large bandwidth input streams and appropriately large computational capacity. Consider vision systems as an example.

Assumptions on the distribution do not count. As soon as the data are taken "off-line" for analysis one has made the data "discrete."

For continuous distribution matching to apply, one must be positioned **constantly** in the event stream and perform all calculations prior to the next occurrence of a meaningful event. This is akin to being in the cylinder of an automobile engine sensing, recording and tracking what happens to each molecule during the combustion cycle.

Having stated all this a distribution comparison is meaningful and the following approximation method can be utilized for an off-line distribution comparison.

The difference of note is in the reassigning of the origin to be positioned at other than the mean of the distribution. Here we will use "left" as the origin.

Statistical techniques do not commonly use left as "best" and right as not best. The difference here is the declaration of a metric of "best." Order statistics are different from unordered statistics. The theory here applies more to "moments." First, second and third moments apply in both the statistical discipline and the engineering discipline.

Consider the case of comparing the information context of two "normal" distributions:

> N (0,1) is a standard normal with mean = 0
> and variance = 1
> N (-1.5, 0.25) is a normal distribution with
> mean = - 1.5 and variance = 0.25

"Best" is defined as being the left origin and worst to the right hand side. The two distributions are aligned relative to the other at the left edge. This is accomplished by matching one unit of the tail (say A_1) of the natural distribution N (0,1). The position of the entropy scale for the N (0,1) is aligned with the first unit of the matching distribution (A_2).

- Draw or calculate distribution function.

- Choose the starting point so that most of the distribution (at least 99%) lies to the right of the starting point and the range from the start (best) to the end (worst) encompasses the distribution.

- Choose the ordinate granularity of the range for the desired number of increments.

- The unit value is then the range divided by the number of increments chosen.

- Calculate the area (A_1) under the distribution for one increment of unit value from the starting point.

- The chance of selecting the best item is the area (A_1). The number of equal probability choices (W_1) is the inverse of the chance (or one divided by the calculated area for the first increment ($W_1 = 1/A_1$)

- The uncertainty in being able to select the best item is $S_1 = -\log_2 W_1$.

- Similarly, for any other comparing distribution, determine its starting point as above.

- Using the unit value previously calculated (step 4) calculate the area under the distribution for one increment of the unit value from the starting point.

- The chance of selecting the best item is this area A_2 given the number of equal chance choices W_2 as $1/A_2$ and corresponding uncertainty as $S_2 = -\log_2 W_2$.

The frequency distribution match is shown below.

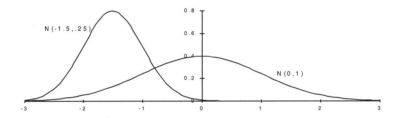

The cumulative distribution and the resulting "S" scale is shown next.

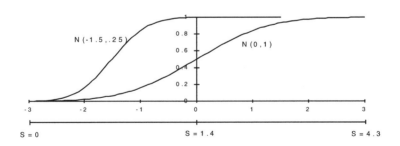

The noteworthy point is the proportion of the distribution biased in the low entropy direction (toward S=0).

Other forms of distributions follow the identical procedure.

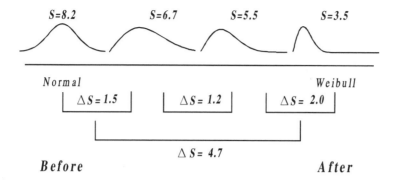

The Variance Method — Rough Starting Approximation

In a variety of cases the underlying distribution is unknown or the data are expensive to obtain. One may not know the entire list of possibilities.

A very good beginning approximation may be achieved by simply using variance. Variance is convenient by virtue of it arriving with two or more data points. Variance is a distribution free statistic. Hence, distribution knowledge is not required. Recall also that variance and entropy are directly linked.

The method is then quite simple.

1. Choose the goal gain ordering statistic and gather two or more measurements or observations.
2. Calculate the variance and standard deviation.
3. Assume that the data will create a standard deviation six times greater than that observed. From this range choose a unit value based on the desired granularity.
4. Choose a log basis (base 2).
5. Spread the range in increments of the unit value from best to worst.

6. In order, the entropy values are calculated as the log of the positional index as 0 to the log of the number of increments.

7. The scale is now complete.

8. Position the current data at the appropriate positional place on the resulting distribution scale. The corresponding entropy value is then estimated.

Example:

Say that three measures are 9.1, 7.8 and 4.5.

Calculate and plot the information content via the variance method for the following small sample.

9.1
7.8
4.5

The method in this case would determine that this sample might be a result of a range from:

$$14.25 \text{ as a high} \qquad (\mu + 3\sigma)$$
$$0.02 \text{ as a low} \qquad (\mu - 3\sigma)$$

The number of segments is arbitrarily assumed to be ten (10) so that a scaled range is created.

The results of positioning the three sample points on the scale is shown below.

sample values				9.1	7.8		4.5			
distribution	14.2	12.7	11.1	9.5	7.9	6.3	4.8	3.2	1.6	0.0
W	1	2	3	4	5	6	7	8	9	10
S	0.00	1.00	1.58	2.00	2.32	2.58	2.81	3.00	3.17	3.32

The information content plot would appear as follows.

Information Content Plot - Variance Method

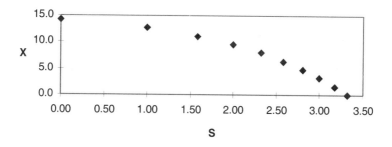

Sensitivity — Confidence

The information entropy scales and computations are quite
sensitive to variance. Sample size does not mean much except
that the extremes of the distribution have not shown. Hence,
the magnitude of the variance is uncertain so that we do not
know how to prescribe the range of possible unique categories.
This dilemma is isolated later.

If, for example, there is an unknowing omission from the
middle of the list then the goal gain entries above where it will
have fallen in order will be unimpacted. The lower items
"below" the missing information will be in error by one positional element.

Similarity in our analysis here we chose to align the highest
goal gain in the sample as "best" with zero entropy. A more
conservative approach could be constructed by assuming the
possibility that several or some percentage of "best" have not
been represented in the sample. Such a thing is easily accom-
modated by adjusting downward "best." The implications of
"tampering" are the same as always.

A most skeptical method is the very small sample as indicated by the Variance Approximation Method. In this method we have attempted to describe the provision as similar to the conservative nature of the "student's T" distribution. Very few samples bring with it the corresponding lack of confidence that the "true" distribution has shown itself. We, the authors, considered eliminating this case as too risky.

On second thought the hypocrisy of measurement in general took precedent. State what exists with certainty and also state the degree of uncertainty (lack of confidence). Given the data, that is the "best" that can be stated with certainty.

A.3   Technique Comparisons

We will now compare the "list" and "distribution" techniques. In so doing, differences are illustrated relating to methods, accuracy and granularity. The selection of $^{Output}/_{Input}$ formulation as the example serves also to expand one of the several most prominent measures that has been described throughout.

Early it was mentioned that we would get close to discovering what fractions are all about. This section is the culmination of that previous statement.

Proper Metrics. If and when metrics are formed from properly describing the ratio of all output in a process divided by all inputs then it is assured that the resulting measure will be a fraction (often a number less than or equal to one). The resulting fraction inherits the character and meaning from what has been composed. The fraction represents the relative completeness of the whole; whatever the components and resultant means to the recipient. Fractional subject knowledge of the topic particulars means limited information.

The treatment here describes intricate, but important, elements. We end by showing how the economic value, information value (EV-IV) measurements and scales relate.

Separable Measures

When **z**, an original ratio measure, is a fraction as it often will be when $^{Out}/_{In}$ is used then it follows that **x** and **y** may be fractions also. One frequently encounters a measure of the form **z** = (**x**)(**y**). Example: $^{Out}/_{In} = ^1/_8 = ^1/_2 \bullet ^1/_4$. The range of the fractions will all be from zero to one. Hence, ranges:

$$\mathbf{z} \qquad 0 \longleftrightarrow 1.0$$
$$\mathbf{x} \qquad 0 \longleftrightarrow 1.0$$
$$\mathbf{y} \qquad 0 \longleftrightarrow 1.0$$

A way to think about this is a pair (**x**,**y**) of ten (10) faced dice. On each face of the die are the numbers in one-tenth increments from 0.1 to 1.0. For the moment, we will omit $^0/_{10}$.

$$\left[\frac{0}{10}\right] \ \frac{1}{10}, \frac{2}{10}, \frac{3}{10}, \frac{4}{10}, \frac{5}{10}, \frac{6}{10}, \frac{7}{10}, \frac{8}{10}, \frac{9}{10}, \frac{10}{10}$$

With each roll of the dice the faces turn up and the two exposed faces are **multiplied** in order to get an answer (**z**).

When these objects are "rolled" the resulting products form a one-hundred (100) cell table of results as follows:

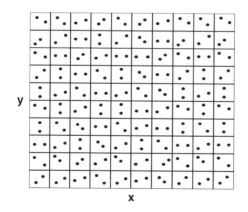

$$\mathbf{z} = \mathbf{x} \bullet \mathbf{y}$$

Each cell in the lattice would be uniformly attended.

Each dot merely represents a "roll"; an observation (in this case 200).

Each cell has the same natural probability of happening,
although as each single event actually "happens" all future
possibilities and anticipation suddenly jump into the reality of
that event outcome. From what we have learned, the amount of
anticipation uncertainty in <u>each</u> cell is $-\frac{1}{100} \log \frac{1}{100} = 0.0664$.
We separate anticipation (potential) from actualization in the
sense that when each event **actually** happens all uncertainty
about that event is resolved. We chose 200 rolls to show that
the "number of rolls" matters not. The amount (quantity) of
data does not matter at all. Data may be measured by weight or
quantity of digits or bits. Valuable information is measured in
goal control degrees.

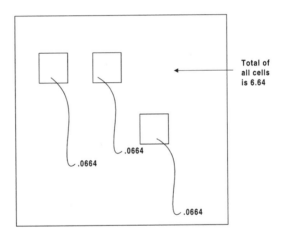

Total of
all cells
is 6.64

The entropic sum of all of the 100 cell possibilities is then 6.64.
This metric represents the maximum (worst case) natural
uncertainty. If the goal is high output for low input, one would
need to find ways to **predestine** the high-end products and
discourage or eliminate the low-end outcomes. Alternately
one would need the **foresight** to bypass the low outcome events
in favor of choosing only the high outcomes. Hence, the
valuable information prerequisite.

It is noteworthy that while **x** and **y** input fractions may "look"
like probabilities because they range from zero to one . . . they
are not. It is best to think of them as objects.

A-34

Recall that the choice was made earlier not to include zero [$^0/_{10}$] faces on the dice. This choice is consequential. Eleven (11) faced dice (including zero) would result in 11 x 11 or 121 possibilities. The uncertainty in each cell would then be $-^1/_{121} \log ^1/_{121} = .0572$. The total for the table would no longer be 6.64. Rather, it would become 6.92. More **choices** create greater **uncertainty**.

A new thing happens when we look at the **z** "product" value ($\mathbf{z} = \mathbf{x} \cdot \mathbf{y}$) in each cell.

x\y	0	0.1	0.2	0.3	0.4	0.5	0.6	0.7	0.8	0.9	1
0	0	0	0	0	0	0	0	0	0	0	0
0.1	0	.01	.02	.03	.04	.05	.06	.07	.08	.09	.10
0.2	0	.02	.04	.06	.08	.10	.12	.14	.16	.18	.20
0.3	0	.03	.06	.09	.12	.15	.18	.21	.24	.27	.30
0.4	0	.04	.08	.12	.16	.20	.24	.28	.32	.36	.40
0.5	0	.05	.10	.15	.20	.25	.30	.35	.40	.45	.50
0.6	0	.06	.12	.18	.24	.30	.36	.42	.48	.54	.60
0.7	0	.07	.14	.21	.28	.35	.42	.49	.56	.63	.70
0.8	0	.08	.16	.24	.32	.40	.48	.56	.64	.72	.80
0.9	0	.09	.18	.27	.36	.45	.54	.63	.72	.81	.90
1	0	.10	.20	.30	.40	.50	.60	.70	.80	.90	1.00

$\Sigma f_{xy} (; x=0,.5, y=0,.6) = $ 3.15   0.105   average $f_{ij}(100) = $ 0.3025

$\Sigma f_{xy} (; x=0,.6, y=0,.5) = $ 3.15   average $f_{ij}(121) = $ 0.2500

The product takes on new values that are different from the original ingredients. The process has transformed the inputs into very different outputs. Whereas the distribution of the horizontal and vertical is uniform, the product result in each cell is far from uniform.

Were one to roll these dice multiple times a frequency distribution would appear. Although each individual die face outcome would be equally likely and each cell pair would be equally likely, the resultant value would NOT have the same chance of appearing. The **z** product chances follow a different distribution.

Terminology and nomenclature note: In the graphical presentations we will use the following:

x	=	upper limit of cell range
f_x	=	frequency count in cell x
p_x	=	probability density of cell x
F_x	=	cumulative probability distribution from 0 to x

f_{xy}	=	frequency count in cell x, y	
S_n	=	$k \log_2 n$	total uncertainty (where n is the number of choices and k is a scaling constant)
S_p	=	S_n/n	cell uncertainty contribution
	=		
$H_\varnothing(m) =$		$-P_\iota \log_2 P_\iota$	(component uncertainty where m denotes the method)
H_m	=	$\Sigma H_\varnothing(m)$	total uncertainty for method m

μ	=	mean	
σ	=	standard deviation	
m'_1	=	1st moment about the origin	
u_i	=	x transform for grouped data moment calculation	
C	=	max $H_m - H_m$ =	certainty measure

We will attempt to hold the nomenclature constant through the remainder of this appendix. It is critical to notice the "shifting distributions" and, in so doing, the changing of the success odds.

The expected result would be:

without ⁰/₁₀

with ⁰/₁₀ included

range	range midpt .0	x	f_x	p_x	F_x
.0-.1	.05	0.1	27	.27	.27
.1-.2	.15	0.2	19	.19	.46
.2-.3	.25	0.3	15	.15	.61
.3-.4	.35	0.4	11	.11	.72
.4-.5	.45	0.5	9	.09	.81
.5-.6	.55	0.6	6	.06	.87
.6-.7	.65	0.7	5	.05	.92
.7-.8	.75	0.8	4	.04	.96
.8-.9	.85	0.9	3	.03	.99
.9-1.0	.95	1	1	.01	1.00
	.55		0	1	
			100		

range	range midpt	x	f_x	p_x	F_x
.0-.1	.05	0.1	48	.40	.40
.1-.2	.15	0.2	19	.16	.55
.2-.3	.25	0.3	15	.12	.68
.3-.4	.35	0.4	11	.09	.77
.4-.5	.45	0.5	9	.07	.84
.5-.6	.55	0.6	6	.05	.89
.6-.7	.65	0.7	5	.04	.93
.7-.8	.75	0.8	4	.03	.97
.8-.9	.85	0.9	3	.02	.99
.9-1.0	.95	1	1	.01	1.00
	.55		0	1	
			121		

Although important, the point here is not so much the value of the ⁰/₁₀. Rather, the inclusion or not substantially alters the characteristics of the outcome. Shortly we intend <u>to reverse this process and remove rather than add faces on the dice</u>. The effect is **profound**. This process forms the fundamental information measurement basis. The frequency distribution of 100 possibilities . . . and 121 possibilities are shown below.

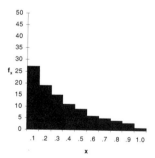

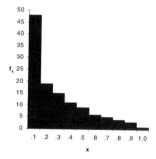

The total uncertainty is still 6.64 but has been reorganized by group. For example, 27 of the 100 possible (0.0664's) are now in the first group. The sum of uncertainty in the high frequency collection is 1.79.

The 21 extra are now included and total to 6.92. The added entries (48) zero results are all in the low range outcome. Forty percent of the expected z outcomes are now 0.1 or less.

Engineers may be interested in the energy units. Notice that in the natural uniform distribution it takes the same amount of energy to generate a 0.1 as it does a 0.9 (the energy involved in one roll). It is not harder in energy terms. It is merely less frequent. It is harder in organizational terms. Unless the process is **controlled** to be other than random, considerable energy is consumed generating "low" outcomes when high outcomes are desired. Twenty-one additional low outcome (zero) possibilities were introduced when the $0/_{10}$ elements were included.

Perhaps one barely noticed the ordering principle that occurred in creating the tables, graphs and distributions. The **order** and **organization** changed when the resultant values combined to cause one end of the listed order, the properties of:

unique, lower frequency, less low gain choices likely, less choice, **more certain**.

To the other end of the listed order, have placed the properties of:

common, high frequency, more low gain choices likely, more choice, **more uncertain**.

Yes, the previous statements are correct. Think about more choices generating less goal gain certainty per choice.

Despite all the numbers being fractions, we have described a multidimensional object. **x, y, z** form a surface that is cone like. As much as anything else we are calculating something that looks like a volume but behaves like a "field force" rather than area or volume. We mention this to draw attention to the engineering aspects of pressure and volume. Our goal is to describe a control surface and we are only part of the way there.

The object being described is illustrated below. When we
multiplied the dice a product mosaic resultant formed. The
resultant **z** is the height of a field vector supporting the surface.

P r o f i l e   o f   z = x · y

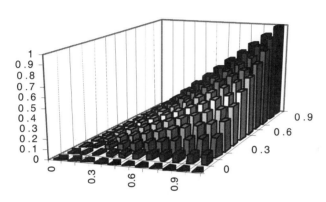

Another topographical form of the resultants:

Top View of z=x·y

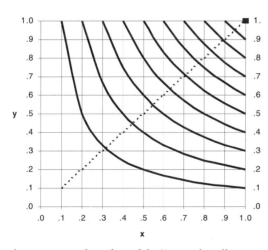

The reader may notice that this "top view" contour form is
similar to weather map pressure gradients, civil engineering
terrainscapes and Return on Investment (ROI). In our way of
thinking the diagrams are almost illustrating information
content alignment.

Whereas the observed probability profile has just been shown, the information profile has not. As explained in the main body of the book and again in this appendix, probability is a **step** on the methodology path to measure goal control surface differences. Earlier in this appendix step 3 and step 5 dictated that the natural and observed entropy be calculated. We show the resulting infoscape profile in the following diagram. The calculations are shown a few pages forward. We are showing the nonlinear shape at this point to illustrate the linear versus nonlinear relationships.

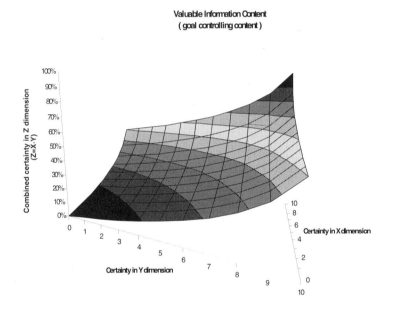

This is perhaps a very first view of a quantified infoscape. The difference is in the nonlinear logarithmic transformation required for information content analysis. Before showing the computations for this **z=x•y** infoscape a few other comments are appropriate for sake of completeness. The question arises about negative numbers left off our dice. Negatives are simply anti-positives.

Negative numbers have not been a part because none were included on the die faces. Had we elected to include minus values then the terrain (**x,y,z**) would have been altered as sketched below.

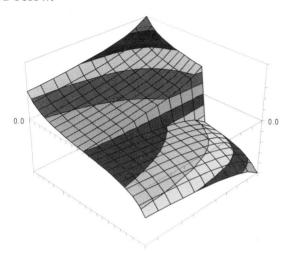

As one can see, the surface becomes multidimensional and nonlinear. A simplification occurs in return on investment because "negative" asset values are ruled out. Therefore, the resulting infospace diagram resembles that shown above. At this point, we prefer not to address this level of complexity but only show what happens.

Rather than pursue the continuing of the quadrants, consider a different thought direction.

See What's Missing. The attempt here will be to describe the essence of information measurement thinking. To do this is somewhat like thinking backwards. Such a thing is simple but not easy. Start a new chain of thought. Think backwards about only observing a single output (**z**) and deducing the inputs (**x** and **y**).

Consider only one single output. For example, you blink and only observed that the product resultant output is 0.3. What are the inputs? Indeterminate! Partly yes and partly no. A better expression is semi-determinant.

What is known for certain is that $1/_{10}$ and $2/_{10}$ were **NOT** a part of the process and neither was $0/_{10}$ if it were included. In fact there are only four ways to obtain a resultant of exactly 0.3.

How can we see this?

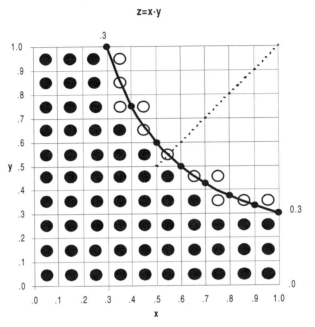

The only ways for exactly 0.3 to appear is for $1/_{10}$ and $2/_{10}$ **NOT** to have played a part. They are **ruled out** of the play. There are only two chances of $3/_{10}$ being a part. There are two ways for $5/_{10}$ and $6/_{10}$ to participate. In fact, none of the black dotted cells below the line or the white cells above could have taken part. Some force ruled these choices out of this singular 0.3 outcome event.

Rather than the "exact" point, consider from here on that 0.3 or greater happens consistently. Outcomes below 0.3 never happen. Consequently, the choices of **x** and **y** where **z** ≥ 0.3 is a much more restricted than previously thought. Only 43 (35.5%) combinations of choices can play a role (the white space). The composition of the 121 outcomes "greater than or equal" include 39 "greater" plus the four (4) "equal" to 0.3.

Statements that we can make about this particular phenomenon consider that the information content that yielded the 0.3 or greater actual resultant was somewhat more **potent** than natural. It was more **restricted**. The **freedom** to choose low gains was less. Control elements predispose a higher product. **Control** is greater in this particular case. The **variation** is less. Someone or something has utilized **an amount** of special or exceptional information to create a higher **degree** of outcome control.

The greater amount of information and control is calculated as

$$\log_2 39 = 5.29 \text{ versus } \log_2 121 = 6.92.$$

There is 1.63 difference in uncertainty from 121 to 39 or an **information content advantage** of 24 percent for the 39 over the 121.

The general case principle attempting to be illustrated considers that properly constructed output versus input measures dually reflect a quantitatively calculable information content. Actually what is happening is reverse. Somewhere in the system **valuable information** is **controlling** the outcomes. Those exhibiting (consistently) the higher output are operating from a different distribution in the exact sense of ruling out inferior natural choices. It is noteworthy that the amount of the superior can be calculated without knowing exactly the detail of "how" the outcome came to be. Return to the "Archer" or your own schooling grades for confirmation.

Business engineers may be inquisitive as to the whereabouts of the energy units that were in the "black dot" region. Where did they go? Nowhere. They were not ever required. The higher outcome product was generated with much less energy usage. The energy for generating all the non 0.3 values (0.0, 0.1, 0.2) was averted. These possibilities were reorganized out of the picture and never happened.

Notice in passing that "value" distances itself from cost at this point. It is not a requirement that more cost be necessary to create valuable outcomes. <u>Quite the reverse is true</u>. Valuable goal gain events require the same or less "cost." The goal gains also happen faster; in less time. The advantageous outcome of faster **and** better **and** cheaper is the consequence of valuable information.

Process engineers and business growth proponents target these outcomes. Higher output for less input is the definition of effectiveness and efficiency. The **direct linkage** to information is a **secret**.

Expressions of Certainty

We now have the building block elements to compare methods.

List Method

The list method can be used to establish a measure of either the semi-determinate line or a specific point on the line depending on which situation presents itself. We will redevelop the 0.3 case as an example using the list method.

Recall the log base 2 uncertainty vector. It contained the following values:

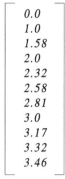

This vector represents cumulative one dimensional uncertainty. Recall also our measurement rule stating that the sum of decomposed uncertainties must "add" up to a composite uncertainty. This design rule is stated on page 97.

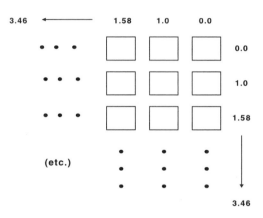

All we need do then is position the vector above on each of the **x** and **y** axis as illustrated above. The list method places the uncertainty vector on each axis at the midpoint of the cell or on the boundary line. The 0.0 uncertainties are positioned at the point of "best" or perfection or goal. In this case it is where $^{Output}/_{Input}$ equal $^1/_1 = 1$. We are not requiring that the goal be one. The goal ratio can be any number or position in the terrain. It is quite interesting to choose other goal targets.

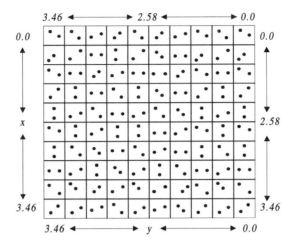

We have now "remapped" and rescaled the space into goal focused infospace. That is all there is to it. We are done. It is that simple.

The total is preserved by summing the **x** and **y** value. The uncertainty of any point is the sum of the **x** and **y** axis uncertainty values. Certainty is merely the "flip" (or complimentary) side of the uncertainty scale.

Whichever positional cell that an actual "**z**" observation occurs becomes the relative certainty. Each axis ranges to 3.46 uncertainty, the sum of which preserves the original 6.92 total.

For the "line" of at least $z = 0.3$ we choose the entry (2.81) in the uncertainty vector scale for **x** and also for **y**. The sum is 5.62. Comparing with the total yields $5.62/6.92 = 0.81$. This means that 81% of the uncertainty remains for those somewhere on the bottom edge of the square shown in the next diagram (at best 19% certain).

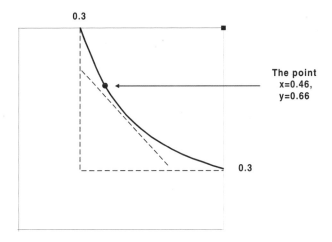

Notice that the dotted square area has been included. We could (and should) refine this approximation by subtracting the triangular area from uncertainty. The amount in the triangle is 1.23. The better estimate for the uncertainty beneath the 0.3 line is 4.39.

The revised statement is:

$$^{4.39}/_{6.92} = 0.63$$

saying that 63% of the uncertainty remains and that 37% is resolved.

Refer back to the previous two pages where the axes have been remapped with the logarithm. For a specific "point" on the 0.3 line (e.g., $\mathbf{x} = 0.46$, $\mathbf{y} = 0.66$) the "$\mathbf{s}$" would be the (2.58) entry on the $\mathbf{x}$ scale and the (2.0) entry on the $\mathbf{y}$ scale. We add these together and determine the relationship to the whole $^{4.58}/_{6.92} = 0.66$. This means that 66% of the uncertainty remains and that the amount of certainty is 34%. No triangle correction is necessary for a point estimate.

Distribution Method

Just as changing from Centigrade to Fahrenheit, we now arbitrarily decide to change scales. The reason and ability to do so is the availability of the method. The H calculation can be accomplished because we know the discrete "distribution" in which the resultant possibilities arrange themselves.

The square (11x11) uncertainty matrix is discarded in favor of a different form. The 6.92 is no longer the measure.

Replacing the 6.92 is an uncertainty vector measure of 2.67 as tabulated below.

range	range midpt	x	f_x	p_x	F_x	$H_i(D)$ i=1,10	cum $H_i(D)$	cum H_i/H_D	u_i
.0-.1	.05	0.1	48	.40	.40	.53	.53	.20	-4.5
.1-.2	.15	0.2	19	.16	.55	.42	.95	.35	-3.5
.2-.3	.25	0.3	15	.12	.68	.37	1.32	.49	-2.5
.3-.4	.35	0.4	11	.09	.77	.31	1.64	.61	-1.5
.4-.5	.45	0.5	9	.07	.84	.28	1.92	.72	-0.5
.5-.6	.55	0.6	6	.05	.89	.21	2.13	.80	0.5
.6-.7	.65	0.7	5	.04	.93	.19	2.32	.87	1.5
.7-.8	.75	0.8	4	.03	.97	.16	2.48	.93	2.5
.8-.9	.85	0.9	3	.02	.99	.13	2.61	.98	3.5
.9-1.0	.95	1	1	.01	1.00	.06	2.67	1.00	4.5
		.55	0	1		2.67 =H_D			0.0
			121					m_1'=	-0.252
									μ=0.30
									σ=0.23

What has happened is the reorganizing and reclassifying of the original 121 event categories into FEWER categories. In this case only ten categories are included.

Care is taken to make certain that all 121 event combinations are included in the ten classes.

If we repeat our analysis of the 0.3 resultant line then the following analysis is provoked.

The 0.3 resultant relating to information thinking is characterized by a **shift** from natural equilibrium. One can think about the case where the $0/_{10}$, $1/_{10}$, and $2/_{10}$ faces were removed from the dice. In fact, all of the choices below the line were ruled out. Refer to the "black dot" graphic.

To see what is **missing** and where the shift actually occurs, the next page analytical method **RETAINS** the exact same scale and method. It is as if the distribution had anticipated with foresight that the $0/_{10}$, $1/_{10}$, and $2/_{10}$ faces were supposed to appear. They did not because of being prevented. The unexpected, in fact, happens!

The resulting "shifted" distribution is described below.

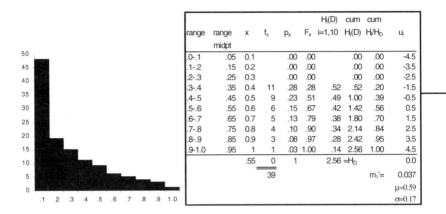

range	range midpt	x	f_x	p_x	F_x	H(D) i=1,10	cum H(D)	cum H/H₀	u_i
.0-.1	.05	0.1		.00	.00		.00	.00	-4.5
.1-.2	.15	0.2		.00	.00		.00	.00	-3.5
.2-.3	.25	0.3		.00	.00		.00	.00	-2.5
.3-.4	.35	0.4	11	.28	.28	.52	.52	.20	-1.5
.4-.5	.45	0.5	9	.23	.51	.49	1.00	.39	-0.5
.5-.6	.55	0.6	6	.15	.67	.42	1 42	.56	0.5
.6-.7	.65	0.7	5	.13	.79	.38	1.80	.70	1.5
.7-.8	.75	0.8	4	.10	.90	.34	2.14	.84	2.5
.8-.9	.85	0.9	3	.08	.97	.28	2.42	.95	3.5
.9-1.0	.95	1	1	.03	1.00	.14	2.56	1.00	4.5
	.55	0		1		2.56 =H₀			0.0
			39					$m_1'=$	0.037
									μ=0.59
									σ=0.17

The amount of the "shift" is illustrated below with respect to the frequency profile differences. The amount of information improvement is the shifting from the left (natural) distribution. The amount of information bias (toward goodness) is the difference.

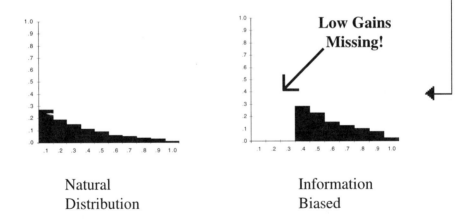

Natural Distribution

Information Biased

Here we see the reasoning for JT defining valuable information as "changing the odds" of positive goal gains. "Somebody is playing from a different set of dice or deck of cards." Refer to the Passenger Overboard example.

Next we shall calculate the information content point estimate
for $x = 0.46$, $y = 0.66$ using the distribution function of z.
Oops! Due to the extreme diligence to independence the
distribution method can no longer calculate a point estimate.
The concept of independence describes z but has yielded
forgetfulness and no memory of the x and y ingredients.

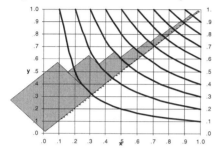

The statistics discipline
has oriented its view
along the diagonal and
"forgets" the ingredients.

Notice that information entropy defines irreversible processes
and is sufficiently **strong** to calculate the control error of
another information system—statistics. It is a powerful information system that can audit other information systems.

The treatment in statistics for determining the x, y effect is
"conditional probability." The section on "Bayes" earlier in
this appendix shows the information relationships.

New Topic. The reader may share a degree of discomfort
regarding how the identical discrete case can result in two
different information content measurement results. They don't.
We do. Each event is discretely unique and like no other. It is
we that choose to categorize. The attempt to arrange . . . in fact
deranges.

The choice of the number and size of the categories (ten) holds
the key. This is the granularity effect. Specificity is another
name for it. When we **reordered** the distribution of (z) outcomes, unlike event outcomes became aggregated. Each of the
ten frequency "buckets" mixed into it substantially unlike
objects. These objects lost their identity of difference in the
doing. Information (perhaps valuable) was lost. The amount
of the content loss is the difference between 3.93 and 2.67.

To regain the information content one must be more precise (finer grained) in the categories. Recall that information and information entropy must necessarily be VERY **sensitive** to variation. It is just exactly that. Nature manufactures "uniqueness" at a rate equal to 6σ. If we care to **see the information differences** we should use category sizes smaller than $\sigma/_6$. The number of categories should then be $6/_\sigma$ or more. Twenty-five is the appropriate number in this case (e.g., $6/_{0.24}$).

The following table recalculates the identical 121 outcomes but organizes into 25 categories rather than ten.

i	$H_i(L)$ $p_i=1/121$ $i=1,121$	cum $H_i(L)$	cum $H_i(L)$ /H_L	x_i	f_x	p_x	F_x	$H_i(D)$ $i=1,25$	cum $H_i(D)$	cum H_i/H_D	u_i
1	1.49 1.49	.21	.04	26	.21	.21	.48	.48	.12	-12
2	.63 2.12	.31	.08	11	.09	.31	.31	.31	.08	-11
3	.86 2.97	.43	.12	15	.12	.43	.37	.37	.10	-10
4	.23 3.20	.46	.16	4	.03	.46	.16	.16	.04	-9
5	.63 3.83	.55	.20	11	.09	.55	.31	.31	.08	-8
6	.34 4.17	.60	.24	6	.05	.60	.21	.21	.05	-7
7	.29 4.46	.64	.28	5	.04	.64	.19	.19	.05	-6
8	.23 4.69	.68	.32	4	.03	.68	.16	.16	.04	-5
9	.29 4.97	.72	.36	5	.04	.72	.19	.19	.05	-4
10	.34 5.32	.77	.40	6	.05	.77	.21	.21	.05	-3
11	.11 5.43	.79	.44	2	.02	.79	.10	.10	.02	-2
12	.23 5.66	.82	.48	4	.03	.82	.16	.16	.04	-1
13	.17 5.83	.84	.52	3	.02	.84	.13	.13	.03	0
14	.23 6.06	.88	.56	4	.03	.88	.16	.16	.04	1
15	.11 6.18	.89	.60	2	.02	.89	.10	.10	.02	2
16	.11 6.29	.91	.64	2	.02	.91	.10	.10	.02	3
17	.06 6.35	.92	.68	1	.01	.92	.06	.06	.01	4
18	.11 6.46	.93	.72	2	.02	.93	.10	.10	.02	5
19	.11 6.58	.95	.76	2	.02	.95	.10	.10	.02	6
20	.11 6.69	.97	.80	2	.02	.97	.10	.10	.02	7
21	.06 6.75	.98	.84	1	.01	.98	.06	.06	.01	8
22	.00 6.75	.98	.88	0	.00	.98	.00	.00	.00	9
23	.11 6.86	.99	.92	2	.02	.99	.10	.10	.02	10
24	.00 6.86	.99	.96	0	.00	.99	.00	.00	.00	11
25	.06 6.92	1.00	1.00	1	.01	1.00	.06	.06	.01	12
	6.92 =H_L		.52	0	1.00		3.93 =H_D			0.0
	$\log_2$ 121= 6.92			121						
	0.0572 =S_p								m_1'= -0.248	
										μ=0.27
										σ=0.24

The following histograms display the very same data (the z outcome possibilities). The only difference is the choice of how many groupings to use. The only difference is 10 versus 25 grouping categories.

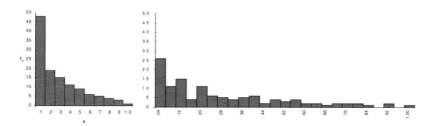

Can you perhaps see where the information ordering and organization principle went astray? Twenty category classes are most appropriate for **x** and **y** because in a uniform distribution $\sigma = \sqrt{1/12}$. Most often ten segments are used (as we did for example). Corrective measures are then applied to adjust for the large granularity. The distribution of **z** while still **ranging** from zero to one was far from uniform and needs 25 classes of distinction.

<u>Shocking Discontinuity</u>. Were we not to have had the discipline strong method or information viewpoint, the missing information would likely have gone unnoticed. Prominent statisticians will argue and "prove" that there is no distortion. Flawed process justifies the end.

The amount of distortion which resulted is medium serious. The uncertainty reduction is 1.26. The "leakage" of the total uncertainty is 47%. Worst of all it is the valuable control information that is lost.

The line of 0.3 along the diagonal is estimable under these conditions. Despite not being able to describe the **x**, **y** contributions the distribution method is easy to use for many single resultant (output side) distribution to distribution entropy comparisons.

The following diagram illustrates the various <u>line</u> intersection uncertainties.

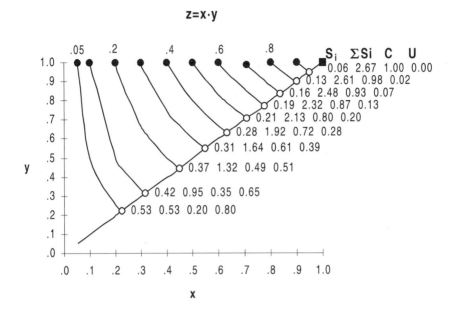

z=x·y

This view has taken a knife and sliced the infospace along the diagonal plane. This graphic precisely describes the diagonal histogram shown previously. The x and y probability axes are connected to entropy (S_i) and the incremental entropies are accumulated in the form of a entropy distribution. Cumulative uncertainty (H) is shown and certainty (C).

Integration - Method

A more precise method is possible because this particular
example has a continuous form complete description. The
successive integration of the control surface possibilities up to
each line represent the probability and uncertainty to that point.
What is happening, in effect, is the expanding of the dice to a
thousand faces of finer granularity. We are no longer solving
exactly the same problem!

The method involves integrating the product equation $z = x * y$
to find the valuable control content in each contour zone. The
zone content relative to the total of the cone represents an
equivalent probability that a uniform choice would fall in to or
out of that cut. The entropy equation is then applied.

In this case the resultant is:

u_i	x	A_x	$p_i=$ dA_x/dx	S_i	cum S_i	H - cum S_i
-5	0	0	0	-p log p	0	2.74
-4	0.1	0.33	0.33	0.53	0.53	2.21
-3	0.2	0.52	0.19	0.46	0.98	1.75
-2	0.3	0.66	0.14	0.40	1.38	1.36
-1	0.4	0.77	0.11	0.34	1.72	1.01
0	0.5	0.85	0.08	0.29	2.01	0.72
1	0.6	0.91	0.06	0.24	2.26	0.48
2	0.7	0.95	0.04	0.20	2.45	0.28
3	0.8	0.98	0.03	0.15	2.60	0.14
4	0.9	0.99	0.02	0.10	2.70	0.04
5	1	1.00	0.01	0.04	2.74	0.00
	0.5 sum		1	H=2.74		
	$m_1'=$	-0.20				
	$\mu=0.30$					
	$\sigma=0.22$					

The total entropy in this case is 2.74.

The uncertainty of the 0.3 "line" is computed to be 0.66. This
is the remaining uncertainty. The certainty is then 0.34.

The "point" $x = 0.46$, $y = 0.66$ lies approximately on the 0.3 line; therefore the point uncertainty is calculated as 0.66.

The resulting equivalent integration for this method is shown below.

$$x \cdot y = c$$
$$y = c/x$$
$$A_c = c + c \int 1/x \, dx \qquad | \int \text{limits are from c to 1}$$
$$A_c = c + c \ln x \, | \qquad | \ln x \, | = \ln x \text{ evaluated from } x = c \text{ to } 1$$
$$A_c = c + c \, (\ln 1 - \ln c)$$
$$A_c = c + c \, (0 - \ln c)$$
$$A_c = c - c \, \ln c$$

Sensitivity Comments

The reader may see that errors of omission are much more prevalent at the base (bottom end) of the all the methods than at the top (complete certainty). One should consider "top down" analysis. It is best to use multiple of the techniques and resolve any differences. This is rather equivalent to the reliability achieved from cross-footing.

The list method is surprisingly simple and durable to abuse. We have abused it here in the interest of simplicity. The surface description analysis 20 x 20 = 400 in the beginning should actually have been considered to be something closer to 10,000 (20 x 20 x 25) choices rather than one hundred twenty-one choices.

The distribution method is troubled by omissions and also by the arbitrary grouping of similar but unequal items. In general it is best to use appropriately grained groupings. The choice to use 25 groups of smaller choice assisted clarity. The rule of thumb which created this was to always use groups of maximum size $\%_6$. The conversion from probability space to infospace is the most critical and most overlooked step.

The unconstrained seeking of greater precision and microscopic granularity is often academic but not economic. A seductive trap is set by the very same law that we are using. Valuable goal gains in business are seeing completely alternate path choices rather than seeing ruts, rocks and smooth spots on a single path. The valuable goal information is more likely to arrive by telescope than microscope.

Time. Notice at this point what has happened to "time" during all these processes. Time is a critical, yet forgotten, ingredient. The time ordered sequence of the results (rolls of the dice) was omitted from all the methods. Had we remembered the order of resultants (in time) we could have detected whether the objects under consideration were **learning** or not to "climb the hill." Time sensitivity is an ingredient which deserves incorporation.

Reliability. Notice in passing that the product form is identical to expressions of reliability. The reliability (of a system) is the product of the time wise stage (**x,y,z**) success—failure ratios. Hence, our choice to describe the very tough reliability example.

Climbing the Uncertainty Hill

$^{Output}/_{Input}$ is a very popular and important measure in business because every process involves the transformation described by the metric. As promised we will end this section by illustrating the EV-IV application of Return On Investment (ROI).

What has been done previous to this point is the separate treatment of the information component from the economic value component. Now, following the methodology (steps 5-8, page 194) we will associate the information and the economic components.

The following graphic depicts the probability hill.

Probability Hill

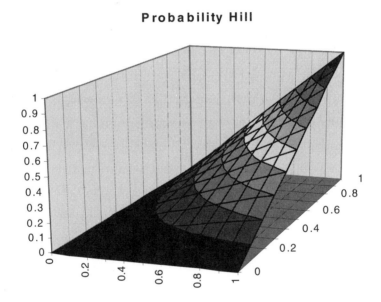

One perhaps senses by now that it is **not** disproportionally harder to have a higher and higher success probability. Intuitively, recall in school that the people that got "A's" did not work harder! The certainty hill seems hard to climb when one is uncertain. Part of the confusion is the nonlinear infoscape. The most severe "hill" is the information hill.

A-58

Here is the same identical hill in information control terms.

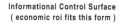

Informational Control Surface
(economic roi fits this form)

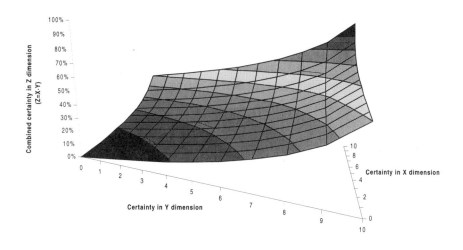

Valuable Information Content

The amount of valuable information content (the goal control amount) is tabulated in the following matrix for the **z=x•y** form.

Shown is the percentage of uncertainty relative to the whole uncertainty of 6.92. The name we assign to this is "information control state matrix." System thinkers may think of this as a knowledge state Markov process. The Information Advantage (beginning on page 366) describes this as a "state space model." The value in each call is the sum of the respective positional **x** and **y** log 2 uncertainty vectors divided by the 6.92 total. The result is expressed as a percentage.

Technically, it is uncertainty that is calculated. Purists would be satisfied by that. The amount of uncertainty that goes away is the amount of information assimilated and the time rate of change at which uncertainty goes away is termed **learning**. The state at any point in time is termed **knowledge**.

Information Control State Matrix
(Valuable Information Content)

		10	9	8	7	6	5	4	3	2	1	0	Low Uncertainty	
		3.46	3.32	3.17	3.00	2.81	2.58	2.32	2.00	1.58	1.00	0.00	0.00	
0	0.00	50.0%	48.0%	45.8%	43.4%	40.6%	37.4%	33.6%	28.9%	22.9%	14.5%	0.0%	0.00	0
1	1.00	64.5%	62.5%	60.3%	57.8%	55.0%	51.8%	48.0%	43.4%	37.4%	28.9%	14.5%	1.00	1
2	1.58	72.9%	70.9%	68.7%	66.3%	63.5%	60.3%	56.5%	51.8%	45.8%	37.4%	22.9%	1.58	2
3	2.00	78.9%	76.9%	74.7%	72.3%	69.5%	66.3%	62.5%	57.8%	51.8%	43.4%	28.9%	2.00	3
4	2.32	83.6%	81.6%	79.4%	76.9%	74.1%	70.9%	67.1%	62.5%	56.5%	48.0%	33.6%	2.32	4
5	2.58	87.4%	85.4%	83.2%	80.7%	77.9%	74.7%	70.9%	66.3%	60.3%	51.8%	37.4%	2.58	5
6	2.81	90.6%	88.6%	86.4%	83.9%	81.2%	77.9%	74.1%	69.5%	63.5%	55.0%	40.6%	2.81	6
7	3.00	93.4%	91.4%	89.2%	86.7%	83.9%	80.7%	76.9%	72.3%	66.3%	57.8%	43.4%	3.00	7
8	3.17	95.8%	93.8%	91.6%	89.2%	86.4%	83.2%	79.4%	74.7%	68.7%	60.3%	45.8%	3.17	8
9	3.32	98.0%	96.0%	93.8%	91.4%	88.6%	85.4%	81.6%	76.9%	70.9%	62.5%	48.0%	3.32	9
10	3.46	100.0%	98.0%	95.8%	93.4%	90.6%	87.4%	83.6%	78.9%	72.9%	64.5%	50.0%	3.46	10
	6.92	3.46	3.32	3.17	3.00	2.81	2.58	2.32	2.00	1.58	1.00	0.00		
	High Uncertainty	10	9	8	7	6	5	4	3	2	1	0		

Although not quite technically pure, **certainty** may be thought of as the complement of uncertainty. For general business purposes it is thought to be suitable. We will show it next.

What these diagrams and numbers show is that when uncertainty goes away, then uncontrol equally goes away. Certainty and control replace uncertainty and uncontrol.

In the two dimensional case (**x,y**) notice that when all of the uncertainty is in one direction, say **x**, then that still leaves half the uncertainty from the other (**y**). Being 100% certain of half the total is still only half certain in TOTAL.

A-60

Information Control State Matrix
(Valuable Information Content)

		0.0	0.1	0.2	0.3	Fractional certainty (p) 0.4	0.5	0.6	0.7	0.8	0.9	1.0	High Certainty
		3.46	3.32	3.17	3.00	2.81	2.58	2.32	2.00	1.58	1.00	0.00	0.00
0.0	0.00	50.0%	52.0%	54.2%	56.6%	59.4%	62.6%	66.4%	71.1%	77.1%	85.5%	100.0%	0.00 1.0
0.1	1.00	35.5%	37.5%	39.7%	42.2%	45.0%	48.2%	52.0%	56.6%	62.6%	71.1%	85.5%	1.00 0.9
0.2	1.58	27.1%	29.1%	31.3%	33.7%	36.5%	39.7%	43.5%	48.2%	54.2%	62.6%	77.1%	1.58 0.8
0.3	2.00	21.1%	23.1%	25.3%	27.7%	30.5%	33.7%	37.5%	42.2%	48.2%	56.6%	71.1%	2.00 0.7
0.4	2.32	16.4%	18.4%	20.6%	23.1%	25.9%	29.1%	32.9%	37.5%	43.5%	52.0%	66.4%	2.32 0.6
0.5	2.58	12.6%	14.6%	16.8%	19.3%	22.1%	25.3%	29.1%	33.7%	39.7%	48.2%	62.6%	2.58 0.5
0.6	2.81	9.4%	11.4%	13.6%	16.1%	18.8%	22.1%	25.9%	30.5%	36.5%	45.0%	59.4%	2.81 0.4
0.7	3.00	6.6%	8.6%	10.8%	13.3%	16.1%	19.3%	23.1%	27.7%	33.7%	42.2%	56.6%	3.00 0.3
0.8	3.17	4.2%	6.2%	8.4%	10.8%	13.6%	16.8%	20.6%	25.3%	31.3%	39.7%	54.2%	3.17 0.2
0.9	3.32	2.0%	4.0%	6.2%	8.6%	11.4%	14.6%	18.4%	23.1%	29.1%	37.5%	52.0%	3.32 0.1
1.0	3.46	0.0%	2.0%	4.2%	6.6%	9.4%	12.6%	16.4%	21.1%	27.1%	35.5%	50.0%	3.46 0.0
Low	6.92	3.46	3.32	3.17	3.00	2.81	2.58	2.32	2.00	1.58	1.00	0.00	
Certainty		1.0	0.9	0.8	0.7	0.6	0.5	0.4	0.3	0.2	0.1	0.0	

(Left axis label: Fractional uncertainty (1-p); Right axis label: Fractional certainty (p))

Fractional uncertainty (1-p)

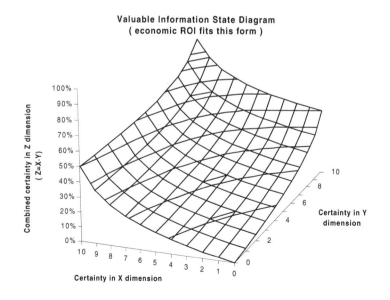

Valuable Information State Diagram
(economic ROI fits this form)

Combined certainty in Z dimension (Z=X·Y)

Certainty in X dimension

Certainty in Y dimension

In the general organization, certainty (0.0 entropy) is placed upper right and, therefore, maximum uncertainty (high entropy) is placed lower left. The inner entropy scale is nonlinear and is mapped to various other linear scales at the proper intercept points.

The outer linear scales represent the fractional certainty (probability) at the top and right sides of a chart and fractional uncertainty (complimentary probability) at the bottom and left sides of a chart.

This technique forms a nomograph that provides graphical translation between the pairs of coordinates and the resultant product in probability terms and entropy terms. A single resultant (e.g., ROI) can be mapped to a contour line (see a few pages hence). If either of the coordinates are known, then the contour can be more precisely positioned.

Rescaling is addressed on page 252 and illustrates how the identical base nomograph can be used with a proper adjustment to wider or narrower scales that are beyond the unit square.

Transfer to ROI – An Application

There are meaningful differences between
  ROI – the investment decision process,
  ROI – the actualization of men, women and machines
        making positive outcomes happen in nature,
  ROI – the control process,
  ROI – the accounting practice of tracking investments,
        and
  ROI – the metric.

The ROI process was conceived with the purpose of improving, if not optimizing, the information content pursuant to contending prospective (future) investment choices. The implementation included a comparison information based alarm control system to detect business critical variation anomalies deserving attention. This is the control process part. The control process part requires information also. This is the accounting practice part.

The metric and measure of ROI is of form $z = x \cdot y$ just presented. The composition of what is included in the $^{Out}/_{In}$ situationally varies.

$$ROI \; = \; ^{Net}/_{Revenue} \; \bullet \; ^{Revenue}/_{Investment} \; = \; ^{Net}/_{Investment}$$

The possibility of negative numbers now enters causing the expansion into other quadrants. The need for the minus one adjustment is shown in the diagram. There is no constant zero.

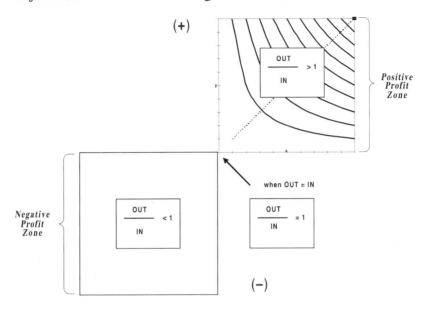

Except for the constant minus one, such a thing is identical to the $^{Output}/_{Input}$ information scale that we have just described. The meaning of the information varies identically with the meaning composed in the ROI form. Not one but **several** measures arise because ROI has multiple forms itself. However, the information scale remains consistent throughout all meanings. The minus one constant does nothing except position the zero point of ROI so that the scale behaves **exactly** like our positive dice.

The predominant parameter here is the (forgotten) "time" component. The various forms of ROI are moving from the prospective anticipation through the actuality of doing to the certainty of history.

The business viewpoint here is an agonizingly S-L-O-W rolling of the dice where ALL men, women and machines in the enterprise are attempting to apply pressure to CONTROL the outcome.

The information content scale forms a simple overlay and rescales the point into information terms. Given a point (ROI), the uncertainty (or certainty) of each axis combines to show the INFORMATION SYSTEMS GOODNESS. The meaning of each axis component is inherited from the definition of ingredients that have been included (e.g., revenue, assets, investment, etc.).

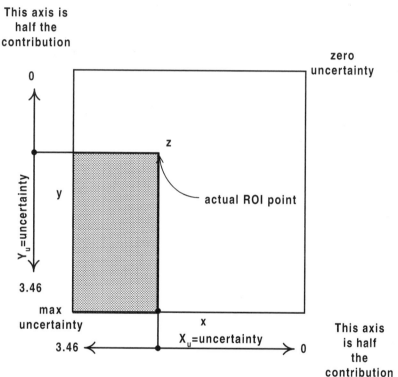

IV = Information Value Scale

The amount of information <u>uncertainty</u>

is $\dfrac{Y_u + X_u}{6.92}$ = IV (ROI$_u$)

IV = Information Value Scale

The amount of information <u>certainty</u>

is $\dfrac{Y_c + X_c}{6.92}$ = IV (ROI$_c$)   where: $Y_c = 1 - Y_u$

and $X_c = 1 - X_u$

A viewpoint can be accomplished by using the "asset" interpretation at the time that the original choice was made to select
it for investment.

Recall how assets become selected in the first place . . . pro-
spectively.

$$Out/_{In} = \frac{\text{Could Have Future Return of This Much (R)}}{\text{By Investing Now This Much (I)}}$$

The decision process dynamics, measures and metrics have
been described in rather full detail elsewhere in this book. The
reliability example (beginning on page 133) is exactly the ROI
decision process. The more general financial view is shown on
pages 81-92.

Little can be added here except to notice that the information to
form the candidate list arises from widespread informed collaboration. An ordering principle is applied to the choice
candidates so that the highest goal gain candidates are illuminated. This ordering is the identical information system that
we used in this section to rule in high output choices and rule
out low return choices. These were the low goal gain omissions ($^0/_{10}$, $^1/_{10}$, etc.) avoided by possessing valuable information. It is also noteworthy that accounting is terrifically rigorous and focused on tracking the choices **made** (the investments) but totally forgets (ignores) any following of choices
NOT made. Hence, the potentially valuable information to
assess and improve the core choice making process is absent.
Recall that this happened here also in the "distribution" method
illustration.

The enterprise has a difficult time answering the question, "Are we actually choosing the highest goal gain paths?"

The metric and measure for the asset investment choice process is sometimes called "performing assets" or "return on assets." In information context one might call this "foresight information systems content" of the enterprise.

The formulation considers that the asset investment event happens. Investments actually happen.

"Time Passes" after investment choices are made. "Potential" begins the actualization process.

$$\frac{\text{Out at Time t}}{\text{In at Previous Time t}} = \frac{\text{Return (to date) + Remaining Future Return}}{\text{Investment (to date) + Remaining Future Investment}}$$

Generally Accepted Accounting Practices (GAAP) happens also. The accounting data are periodically available to carefully construct:

$$\frac{\text{Net Income}}{\text{Revenue}} \bullet \frac{\text{Revenue}}{\text{ASSETS}} \Leftarrow$$

This is our familiar form of $z = x \bullet z$. A measure of short term (expense) choices and longer term (asset) choices is the result.

The various formulas for Return on Investment are:

$$ROI = \frac{R - E}{R} \bullet \frac{R}{I} = \frac{R - E}{I} = \frac{OUT \ (Net)}{IN \ (Total)}$$

The investment term (I) usually represents total investment and when assets are being specifically considered "A" for asset investment is substituted in the position of (I).

Given proper construct the contextual information content can be diagrammed in a time track as illustrated.

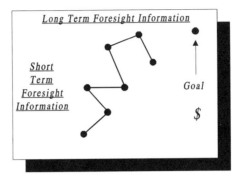

Foresight Information Systems

The vertical axis represents short term expense and revenue performance choices and the horizontal axis represents longer term asset performance anticipation choices. Collectively a context becomes the balance of foresight information systems that are operating in the enterprise. The book, Ahead of Time, expands this view in greater depth. The high foresight enterprise capitalizes information by selecting to invest in ONLY the high outcome futures.

This view represents a measure of the amount of valuable information used by the collective investment choice makers in the enterprise. At the enterprise level the measure is holistic. Every business choice of every participant is included.

Reenter the variable meaning accounting practice of ROI. Periodically (quarterly, annually) the accounting group applies their best (tax code biased) judgment as to the degree in which assets have been consumed. An accumulation is made so that "E" represents the best estimator of the total expense.

Next consider the various alternative forms of the ROI measure.

$$ \text{ROI} \quad = \quad \frac{R - E}{R} \cdot \frac{R}{E} \quad = \quad \frac{R - E}{E} \quad = \quad \frac{R}{E} - 1 \quad = \quad \frac{\text{Out}}{\text{In}} - 1 $$

This particular form follows a similar pattern but assets have disappeared to be considered "expenses."

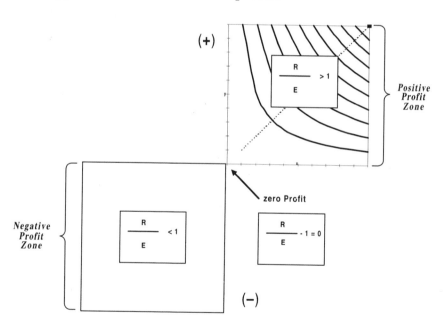

The amount of R/E greater than zero again behaves exactly to the infospace template. The meaning is different.

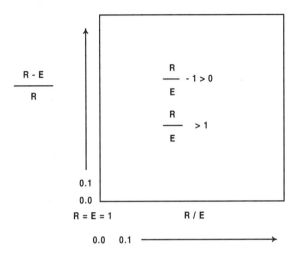

Meaning of the Output/Input

The enterprise possesses Valuable Information about how to efficiently transform expense into revenue (production). The net result is profit.

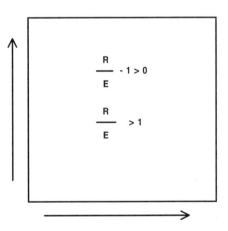

The enterprise possesses Valuable Information about how to select and compose expense (Inputs) that generate revenue {through marketplace products and services}.

A-70

Example

There are several choices for determining the information associated ROI "goodness" measure. One way would be similar to the "Archer." The measure of information impact would be the distance of a line plotted from either the lower left or upper right corner of the graph to the actual ROI point placed in the composite graphical overlay. While this method is very insightful, it does not resolve the matching and synchronizing of the measurement scales we seek.

Measurement Scaling. For this application we first need to substitute the actual formulation.

$$y = \frac{R\text{-}E}{R}$$

$$x = \frac{R}{E}$$

$$z = \text{Resultant}$$

The scale can be configured by selecting a target **z** resultant. The derived scale that has been developed to this point is a **square** display where all end points are one (1.0).

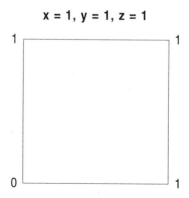

x = 1, y = 1, z = 1

The overlaying of scales yields a resulting tableau shown in the following diagram. This overlay will be the basis of integrating the information content measure with the corresponding economic measure.

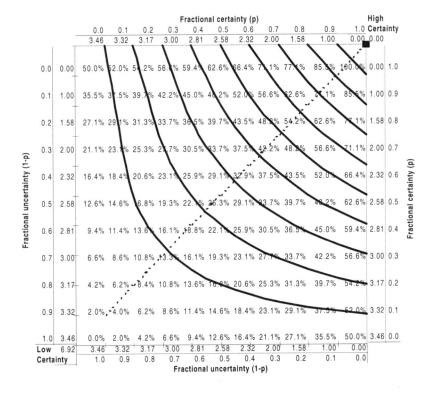

So long as the relationship of **x•y=z** is retained, the end points on the scale can be adapted to bound the range exhibited in the actual data.

For example:

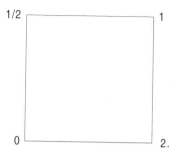

The boundary relationship
holds for the scale of
$y = \frac{1}{2}$ and $x = 2$.

We have held the upper right point constant at one (1.0).

The adjoining example
holds for the scale of
$y = \frac{1}{4}$ and $x = 4$.

Notice, however, that in holding the shape of a square, what otherwise would have been a rectangle has been compacted or stretched (sometimes called "morphing"). Care must be exercised to maintain synchronization of the other associated scales as well as the internal points.

The example enterprise data we shall use is shown on page 164. The scale ranges which satisfy the boundary relationships for the two end points are

$$\frac{R\text{-}E}{R} = 0.5 \quad \text{(y axis scale)}$$

$$\frac{R}{E} = 2.0 \quad \text{(x axis scale)}$$

Therefore, our **x** and **y** goal scale range is now determined in the range. The **x** scale ranges from 0.0 to 2.0 while the **y** scale ranges from 0.0 to 0.5. The several scales can now be aligned for the overlay definition. We can now overlay the information control state matrix with the resultant ROI example actuals and create an information system value comparison. For this illustration we shall "certainty" view of the matrix.

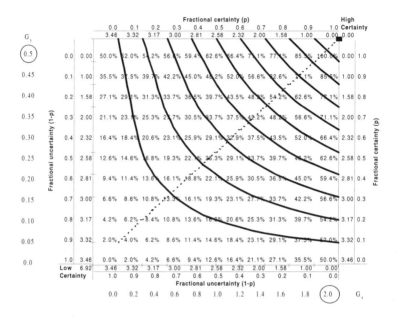

Page 164 shows typical data for an example enterprise. A line (partial) representing the **z**=0.05 has been added. The "expense" version plot of an example company follows:

1.   ıo plot the position of the example, select the 1990 revenue over expense value of 1.053. This is the **x** axis goal coordinate.

2.   The corresponding **y** goal coordinate for 1990 is net return divided by revenue of 0.05.

3.   The (**z**) expense version of ROI is 0.053.

4.   Note that the scale will need to be adjusted to **y**=1/2, **x**=2.0 as shown on page 250 and 251.

Top View of z=x·y

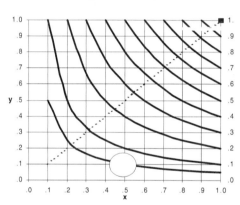

The circle on the chart represents the position of the 1990 point for this enterprise. The remainder of points for this particular enterprise fall in the same zone. This enterprise is not dynamic. The control is tight. Rescaling shows finer differences.

Valuable Information Measures

Number of Valuable Information Units	=	1.02
Percent of Example Enterprise Goal Control	=	14.7%
Example Enterprise Information Worth	=	$5,798*

*Beyond cost and above natural equilibrium. This worth is undervalued by an amount equal to the sum of customer goal gains derived from using the information content transferred through example enterprise offerings (non-physical ingredients exchanged). Customer oriented value ledgers are required to complete the recursive information valuation process.

The amount of goal controlled (valuable) information in the cell region approximates 15% certainty. The vertical y axis contribution is 2% and the remainder is x axis.

Next we will address the example enterprise "asset" view and add that view to the time track diagram. This step returns us to the foresight discussion a few pages earlier.

The vertical axis remains unaffected by this change. It is the horizontal (**x**) axis that is altered. The shape and form of the diagram remain stable so long as the formula does not change. The range of the scale may need alteration because of the size of the numbers representing the "asset" investments. Recall that these data represent the collection of all future decided investment action commitments.

Whereas the **x** axis scale of two represented a short period of time, the asset view may represent four, eight or more years. For illustration purposes here we stay consistent with the **z** product of one (1.0). We shall expand the **x** axis to eight causing the **y** axis to become one-eighth. The plotting of the asset view results in the following diagram.

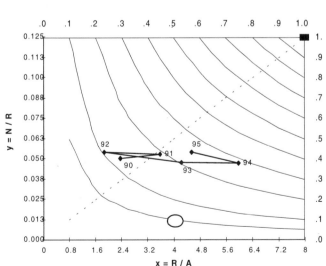

Top View of z=x·y

The information metrics resulting from the combined scale result in the following.

Valuable Information Measures

	Yr.	Units
The list shown at right depicts the number of units of valuable information associated with each year for the example. The content units are either calculated from the formula given or "lifted" from the overlay diagrams.	90	1.14
	91	1.32
	92	1.14
	93	1.57
	94	2.23
	95	1.53

The valuation or worth of the information units shown above is represented in the table below. For each year the certainty (C) is shown along with the ROI. A new ROI (equilibrium) is calculated or "lifted" from the infospace diagrams. This represents the amount of natural equilibrium expected. In this example years 90-94 were below expectation and thus constitute an information deficiency relative to natural. The last year (95) results in a positive or "valuable" increase in information content.

yr	C	ROI	$=ROI_E$	$ROI-ROI_E$	$info
90	1.14	0.118	0.165	-0.047	$ (2,297)
91	1.32	0.188	0.191	-0.003	$ (146)
92	1.14	0.101	0.165	-0.064	$ (3,451)
93	1.565	0.201	0.226	-0.026	$ (1,755)
94	2.225	0.282	0.322	-0.040	$ (3,580)
95	1.53	0.244	0.221	0.023	$ 2,025

Example Summary

It has not been the intent here to examine the detail development of the entire ROI concept. Rather, our goal has been to illustrate a method of measuring the information content within the ROI frame and context. There are many issues for the serious reader to resolve.

Recall the perpetual motion discussion in the body of the book. Return (output) cannot be greater than input (investment). Yet, throughout this example returns exceeded investment. A second point concerns the seemingly direct linkage between "assets" and the WHOLE of net return. The interpretation yields the conclusion that it is these and only these assets which produce profitability. Such is an untruth.

We suggest that the resolution lies in the large understatement of investment caused by the restricted rules of what can be a value generating and performing asset. The dynamics of time sensitivity between what is past and what is future magnify the complexity.

ROI Example Monetization

The reader should be better able now to understand the earlier definition of valuable information. If an enterprise is operating at our 0.3 ROI level, then information about 0.2 is <u>not</u> valuable because it <u>does not</u> represent a <u>positive goal gain</u>. To the enterprise that is 0.1 ROI the **very same** information is valuable because it does represent a positive goal gain.

Given that there are 6.92 units of information in the positive value zone, an enterprise can compute the value (to them) of a unit of ROI information certainty or uncertainty. The semantic equivalent is information system value. One only needs to read the overlaid scale for ROI to find the units of valuable information and then scale the dollars appropriately.

A-78

In "real life" operational terms the enterprise cannot **control** ROI upward until and unless valuable information relating to ROI is available and **used** resulting in higher goal gains. The low ROI choices must be **eliminated** in favor of **high** ROI **choices**. The **absolute** requirement is the information (system) to do it. The value of the information is the value of the resulting positive ROI differential. The monetized value may be expressed in any of the terms composing ROI such as net income, revenue, expense or return on investment. As shown in the reliability example, a unit of valuable information may be stated to be worth the associated amount of profitability.

Methodology Review

The perception and diligent reader may observe what has happened in the pages starting with page 210 "Technique Comparison." What actually was accomplished involved a rapid paced implementation of the methodology itself. We accomplished a recursive process that developed the methodology by using the methodology. Notice if you will that very few methodologies are sufficiently powerful to define their own ending state. Such is the case with genuinely primitive measures. It was simple. Information is controlling!

With the dice scenario, we developed the natural equilibrium scenario which constitutes the first four steps in the method. Next we adopted the actual data (the ROI application and example). These are steps five through seven. Then we associated the economic value impact. It is not a hypocritical methodology. Rather it is powerfully fundamental. We have the origin here of a primitive measure of the highest degree!

Tracker Diagram (EV-IV and More)

The powerful visual simplicity of the
"tracker" diagrams accelerate the
understanding of the otherwise very
difficult to comprehend infospace.
We suppose such a thing is always
appreciated when presented with
duality. Tracker diagrams are much
more than duality and deserve note.

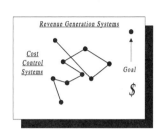

The ability to represent components, resultants, actions, information, economic impact
and time in the same graphic is impressive.
In technical terms the time tracker diagrams
could be described as othogonal info-
economic space time diagrams. These type
diagrams and their descendants may become
as important to economic cyberspace as the
perspective view engineering drawing was to
the industrial age.

Two faces?

A Vase?

The diagrams also represent "holography." What this means is
whole story or whole message in a single space time diagram.
Holospatial and holotemporal combine as a static form of
holodynamic. The connectedness of the holotemporal tracker
is such that any time wise component change resonates
throughout. Any disconnects are noticeable.

Pioneers in "new" physics describe a four-dimension action
oriented world view. This is our best attempt to pictorially
represent the four dimensions in flat two dimensional space.

Other Metrics — Caution

We have developed here **only one** form of information value
metric. This single $^{Out}/_{In}$ metric is important but in no way

represents the totality of business measures. $^{Out}/_{In}$ measures cascade to all processes, however large or small. As a consequence the information content of any or every process is measurable in this way. Often the input is unknown. "Output only" measures (effectiveness) are different. Each metric must undergo similar rigor. Although the introductory reader may consider this extremely complex and rigorous . . . it is not. The academic community could call this coarse, rough and casual. Our intention is a tip of the iceberg treatment. The wrongs will be discovered and corrected. This will be good. We can only hope that it is the young students rather than the masters who detect and correct any illnesses found herein! The masters will appreciate this approach.

Information Economics — Information Engineering

A point in closing considers a frustrating confrontation that bumps into information engineers, value engineers and valuable information proponents. The debate inevitably arises whether these infoscape measurements and metrics should "FOLLOW" accounting practices. To the information engineer the question is nonsense. All of accounting is nothing else but an information system. There is nothing more or less to accounting. Therefore, it is incumbent on the accounting system to "FOLLOW" best information practices.

Other emerging information engineering disciplines such as Chaos Theory, Artificial Intelligence and Fuzzy Logic are addressing the identical issues. Each of these creates a separate unique and secret coded vocabulary so as to start from a clean beginning and also to disguise the issues and avoid the confrontations. We have not done that here despite wanting to. The proof in all this provable pudding relates to appreciating the high goal gain information . . . valuable information.

APPENDIX B
INFORMATION POWER

Briefing
Sessions

Detailed Working
Sessions

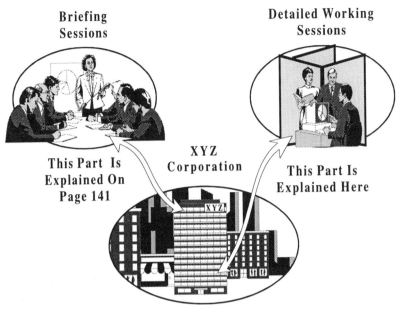

This Part Is
Explained On
Page 141

XYZ
Corporation

This Part Is
Explained Here

The Reader Will Be Required To
Bounce Back And Forth . . . Just
Like Real Life Activities

Main Case
Flow Sequence

Appendix B

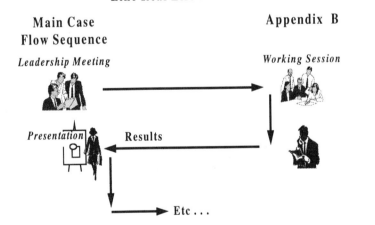

Leadership Meeting

Presentation   Results

Working Session

Etc . . .

B.   *Constructs of Reliability*

Reliability is a good approach for practicing and learning about information entropy. The advantage is the ability to perform economically consequential daily activities and simultaneously develop information optimization skills. Reliability deals with odds and probabilities and systems and distributions and success - failure criteria and economic consequences. Reliability provokes understanding of dynamic stochastic systems. Systems of business are dynamic stochastic systems.

The point here is to demonstrate the information content improvement in a "black box" system that might be all machines, all people or a mix.

Redundancy Design Choices

The inclusion of redundancy to improve reliability can be configured in two differing ways — simple active and standby. For our case example we chose to display <u>standby</u> component units as opposed to completely redundant production "lines." The alternative method is briefly described below even though it is **not** the one developed in the scenario. <u>The "information" relevant point being made here is that the designers **choice** of solution methods alters the outcome.</u>

Simple Active Redundancy

The reliability of a system containing simple active redundancy is estimated using either equation below. In the discrete case reliability can be determined using the probability that the components are operating successfully:

$$R = [1 - (1 - p)^n]^m$$

or in the continuous case using the failure rate:

$$R(t) = [1 - [1 - e^{-\lambda t}]^n]^m$$

where p is the probability of success, n is the number of parallel elements, m is the number of subsystems, and λ is the failure rate.

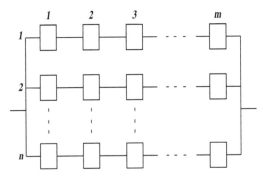

The "team" <u>did not choose</u> this configuration of redundancy because it would have configured entire redundant production lines rather than components.

The Case Choice

The alternative selected (Configuration 1, 2, etc.) contains
standby component redundancy with perfect switching (failures are due entirely to component failures and not to a switching failure). The reliability function for component standby
redundancy is:

$$R(t) = \sum_{k=0}^{n-1} e^{-\lambda t}(\lambda t)^k / k!$$

where n is the number of components required for the assem-
bly to function, λ is the failure rate, and n is the number of
parallel components.

The mean time to failure is reported in this case study and can
be found by:

$$MTTF = n/\lambda$$

Differences and Considerations

In standby the alternate unit is "switched" into service upon the
failure of the currently active unit. In simple active systems
the capacity is essentially multiplied to the point that performance can shift or be absorbed by an alternate unit during a
unit outage. In the context of man/machine systems the idea of
standby may seem peculiar. The idea of one human waiting at
idle for an outage is hard to imagine, for example. However,
when alternate skills are considered or consultants/temporaries
it is easier to consider the configurations.

B.1   *Establishing Reliability Options*

As a result of the initial meeting of the XYZ Corporation, the reliability engineer, in an off-line mode, develops a reliability improvement approach. Realizing that the objective is to choose the highest return on reliability given cost restraints, she validates and reevaluates the failure data and determines the appropriate distribution. Here are the details of her inquiry:

Base (Current) System

The base system is a simple serial system with one component per stage. System reliability is dependent on the individual component reliabilities within each stage. The component reliability (λ = failure rate) and its unit cost per month is included in the figure below.

System 1

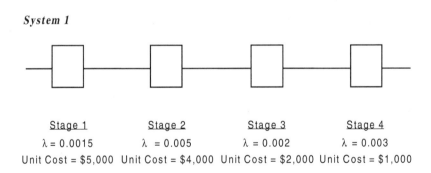

Stage 1	Stage 2	Stage 3	Stage 4
$\lambda = 0.0015$	$\lambda = 0.005$	$\lambda = 0.002$	$\lambda = 0.003$
Unit Cost = $5,000	Unit Cost = $4,000	Unit Cost = $2,000	Unit Cost = $1,000

Stage 1[41]

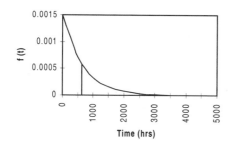

The Stage 1 component has a unit cost of $5,000 and a failure rate, λ, of 0.0015/hour. The resulting mean time to failure[42] for this component is 667 hours.

Stage 2

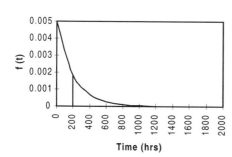

The failure rate for the Stage 2 component is 0.005/hr. It has a higher failure rate than the component in Stage 1, which means that it, in addition to the system, has a higher probability of failure. The unit cost for this component is $4,000 and has a mean time to failure of 200 hours.

---

[41]   The exponential density function is appropriate to model component in a serial system when the failures are considered to be random. The function is:

$$f(t) = \lambda e^{-\lambda t} \quad \text{Where } t = time$$

$$\lambda_{components} = 1/MTTF$$

Note: A serial system is any system with one component/stage. Any one component failure (which is the same as any one stage failure) causes the system to fail.

[42]   Mean time to failure (MTTF) = 1 / failure rate = $1/\lambda$. The graphical diagrams illustrate the timewise density diagram for the constant λ failure rate. The vertical line in the diagram depicts the expected time to failure (MTTF).

Stage 3

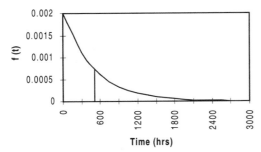

The component in Stage 3 has a failure rate of 0.002/hr and a unit cost of $2,000. The mean time to failure is 500 hours.

Stage 4

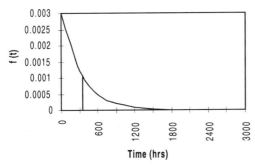

The failure rate for the last stage is 0.003/hr. It has a unit cost of $1,000 and a mean time to failure of 333 hours.

Base System Reliability Summary

The system characteristics are the net results of the components. The resulting system failure rate, λ_s, is 0.0115 per hour and the mean time to failure is 87 hours. The total monthly cost for this system is $12,000.

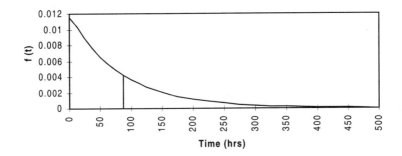

Redundant System

The reliability engineer next needs to decide, based on time and level of detail, what to present at the <u>first</u> meeting. The decision is made to present only two introductory topics. These are:

a) A system view

and

b) The case of equal redundancy

The basis for this choice is the knowledge from experience that introduction precedes detail. The exact configuration will require cost and benefit calculation.

Redundant System

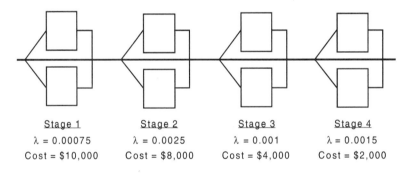

Stage 1	Stage 2	Stage 3	Stage 4
$\lambda = 0.00075$	$\lambda = 0.0025$	$\lambda = 0.001$	$\lambda = 0.0015$
Cost = $10,000	Cost = $8,000	Cost = $4,000	Cost = $2,000

Stage 1[43]

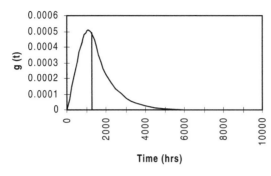

The failure rate for Stage 1 is now 0.00075/hr. The resulting mean time to failure is 1333 hours. The total cost for this stage is $10,000.

Stage 2

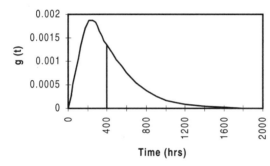

The failure rate for Stage 2 is 0.0025/hr. The mean time to failure is 400. Total cost for Stage 2 is $8,000.

---

[43]   The gamma distribution is appropriate to model stage failure in a parallel system when the failure density is assumed to be exponential and the components are identical. The gamma density function is:

$$g(t) = \frac{\lambda}{(n-1)!} (\lambda t)^{n-1} e^{-\lambda t}$$

Where t = time

λ components = $1/MTTF$

n = # of components

Note: A parallel system is any system where stages contain multiple redundant components. Notice when $n=1$, $g(t)$ reduces to the previously discussed exponential function $f(t)$.

Stage 3

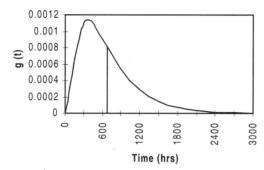

The failure rate for Stage 3 is 0.001/hr and the stage has a mean time to failure of 1000 hours. This stage has a combined cost of $4,000.

Stage 4

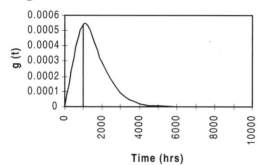

The failure rate for Stage 4 is 0.0015/hr and has a mean time to failure of 667 hours. This stage costs $2,000.

Redundant System Reliability Summary

The resulting system failure rate for the system with one redundant component added to each stage is 0.00575 per hour and the mean time to failure is 174 hours. The monthly cost for the entire system is $24,000.

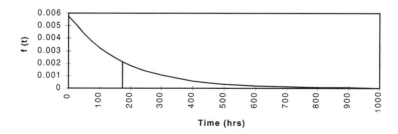

This system along with the base will be subsequently presented. Activity in B.2 is engaged in anticipation.

B.2   Improving the Base System

The next task is the specific choice of alternatives to propose. This section identifies the activities pursuant to the choices.

The failures are caused by component parts with high failure rates that contribute to an unacceptable total system failure rate. The failure rate can be lowered by adding redundant parts or by increasing the reliability of the components. Both approaches increase the cost of the system. The finance department will allow an investment of up to $8,000 to improve the reliability of the system.

The following table lists alternative configurations available to the systems engineer given an addition of up to $8,000 beyond the single component configuration. The knowledge that the reliability engineer had about reliability allowed her to determine the optimum configuration to maximize reliability at a given cost level.

unit cost =	$5,000	$4,000	$2,000	$1,000		prod.hrs = 720
MTTF =	667	200	500	333		(monthly)

Choice #	Stage 1	Stage 2	Stage 3	Stage 4	MTTF	Cost
1 (Base)	1	1	1	1	86	$12,000
2	1	1	1	2	99	$13,000
3	1	1	2	1	95	$14,000
4	1	1	1	3	105	$14,000
5	1	1	1	4	108	$15,000
6	1	1	2	2	111	$15,000
7	1	1	3	1	98	$16,000
8	1	1	1	5	109	$16,000
9	1	2	1	1	111	$16,000
10	1	1	2	3	117	$16,000
11	2	1	1	1	93	$17,000
12	1	1	1	6	111	$17,000
13	1	1	3	2	115	$17,000
14	1	1	2	4	121	$17,000
15	1	2	1	2	133	$17,000
16	1	1	4	1	99	$18,000
17	2	1	1	2	108	$18,000
18	1	1	1	7	112	$18,000
19	1	1	3	3	122	$18,000
20	1	1	2	5	123	$18,000
21	1	2	2	1	124	$18,000
22	1	2	1	3	142	$18,000
23	2	1	2	1	102	$19,000
24	1	1	1	8	112	$19,000
25	2	1	1	3	114	$19,000
26	1	1	4	2	117	$19,000
27	1	1	2	6	125	$19,000
28	1	1	3	4	126	$19,000
29	1	2	1	4	148	$19,000
30	1	2	2	2	153	$19,000
31	1	1	5	1	100	$20,000
32	1	1	1	9	113	$20,000
33	2	1	1	4	117	$20,000
34	2	1	2	2	121	$20,000
35	1	3	1	1	122	$20,000
36	1	1	4	3	124	$20,000
37	1	1	2	7	126	$20,000
38	1	1	3	5	128	$20,000
39	1	2	3	1	130	$20,000
40	1	2	1	5	151	$20,000
41	1	2	2	3	166	$20,000

Configuration 1 - Option

Configuration 1 (choice 35) is a variation of the base system with multiple components in Stage 2 acting as standby units. It places the redundant components in the stage with the highest failure rate. The extra components in Stage 2 are standby units that are not activated until a companion unit fails. These units add redundancy to the system and increase its cost but the reliability of the system is also increased.

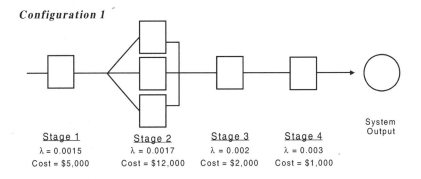

Configuration 1

Stage 1	Stage 2	Stage 3	Stage 4	System Output
λ = 0.0015	λ = 0.0017	λ = 0.002	λ = 0.003	
Cost = $5,000	Cost = $12,000	Cost = $2,000	Cost = $1,000	

Configuration 1 - Summary (System View)

The failure rate for the entire system is 0.00820 with a mean time to failure of 122 hours. The total monthly cost for Configuration 1 is $20,000. By increasing the number of components (adding redundancy) in the least reliable segment of the system, the mean time to failure is increased by 36 hours at a cost of $8,000. The reengineering of the system improved the reliability.

There are six alternate choices that improve mean time to failure over Configuration 1 at the same monthly cost of $20,000. By ordering the table according to increasing cost, the configuration with the highest mean time to failure can be chosen for a particular cost level. In this case, choice 41 was chosen as Configuration 2.

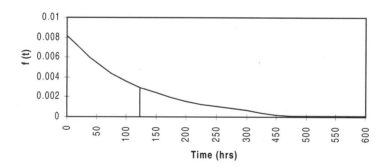

Configuration 2

Configuration 2 (choice 41) is also a variation of the base system with multiple components in three of the four stages. As in Configuration 1, a standby unit is activated upon the failure of the companion.

Configuration 2

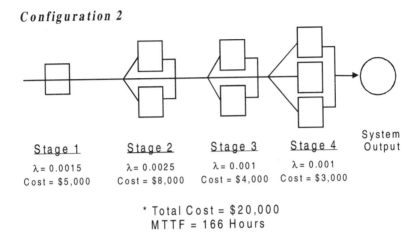

				System
Stage 1	Stage 2	Stage 3	Stage 4	Output
λ = 0.0015	λ = 0.0025	λ = 0.001	λ = 0.001	
Cost = $5,000	Cost = $8,000	Cost = $4,000	Cost = $3,000	

* Total Cost = $20,000
MTTF = 166 Hours

Configuration 2 Summary (System View)

The system failure rate is 0.006 with a mean time to failure of 166 hours. The mean time to failure is increased by 45 hours over Configuration 1 with the same investment of $8,000.

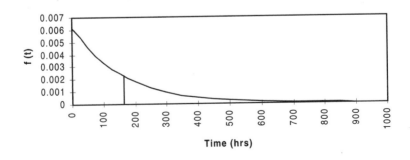

The result of implementing the second proposal is a further increase in the system reliability. Production and profits are also increased over Configuration 1. The reliability improves more when the entire system was taken into account rather than a single stage (lowest component reliability).

The critical feature driving the system's reliability and cost, therefore, is the placement of redundant components throughout the system.

Alternative Comparison

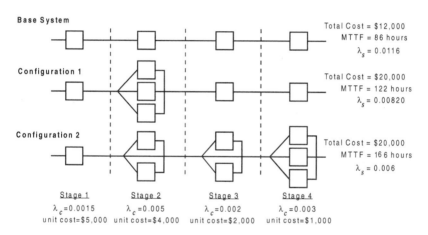

Base System

Total Cost = $12,000
MTTF = 86 hours
λ_s = 0.0116

Configuration 1

Total Cost = $20,000
MTTF = 122 hours
λ_s = 0.00820

Configuration 2

Total Cost = $20,000
MTTF = 166 hours
λ_s = 0.006

Stage 1
λ_c=0.0015
unit cost=$5,000

Stage 2
λ_c=0.005
unit cost=$4,000

Stage 3
λ_c=0.002
unit cost=$2,000

Stage 4
λ_c=0.003
unit cost=$1,000

The base system was a least cost configuration. That system minimized the total cost, but in doing so the reliability of the system also was minimized and caused consequences in the outcomes.

In Configuration 1, the number of components in Stage 2 was increased to three. This configuration increased reliability and, therefore, positively impacted production and profits, but the system reliability was not maximized with the $8,000 investment (as evidenced by Configuration 2).

Configuration 2 represented a systems approach to improving reliability. At a total cost of $20,000, the system failure rate was decreased to 0.006. Configuration 2 was able to increase its mean time to failure by 81 hours at a cost of $8,000 over the base system. Configuration 2 was also able to increase its mean time to failure over Configuration 1 at the same total cost.

Significant Observations

Notice that the improvement is rather "blind" unless measurement is accomplished at the system level. A measure is required to balance the conflicting objectives of cost versus reliability. This observation is a restatement of operations research optimization theory (i.e., maximizing the stages individually does not guarantee systems wide optimum). The point here is that WHERE the system engineer chooses to measure makes a difference.

Let's examine the previous table again but this time add information about the expected number of failures. The number of failures is found by dividing the production hours by the mean time to failure. Because any fraction of a failure means that the whole system will fail, all numbers are rounded up to the nearest integer.

The table now shows that alternatives 29, 30, 40 and 41 will likely encounter five system outages, but alternatives 29 and 30 are $1,000 less.

unit cost =	$5,000	$4,000	$2,000	$1,000		prod.hrs =	720
MTTF =	667	200	500	333		(monthly)	

Choice #	Stage 1	Stage 2	Stage 3	Stage 4	MTTF	Failures	Cost
1 (Base)	1	1	1	1	86	9	$12,000
2	1	1	1	2	99	8	$13,000
3	1	1	2	1	95	8	$14,000
7	1	1	3	1	98	8	$16,000
11	2	1	1	1	93	8	$17,000
16	1	1	4	1	99	8	$18,000
23	2	1	2	1	102	8	$19,000
31	1	1	5	1	100	8	$20,000
4	1	1	1	3	105	7	$14,000
5	1	1	1	4	108	7	$15,000
6	1	1	2	2	111	7	$15,000
8	1	1	1	5	109	7	$16,000
9	1	2	1	1	111	7	$16,000
10	1	1	2	3	117	7	$16,000
12	1	1	1	6	111	7	$17,000
13	1	1	3	2	115	7	$17,000
17	2	1	1	2	108	7	$18,000
18	1	1	1	7	112	7	$18,000
24	1	1	1	8	112	7	$19,000
25	2	1	1	3	114	7	$19,000
26	1	1	4	2	117	7	$19,000
32	1	1	1	9	113	7	$20,000
33	2	1	1	4	117	7	$20,000
14	1	1	2	4	121	6	$17,000
15	1	2	1	2	133	6	$17,000
19	1	1	3	3	122	6	$18,000
20	1	1	2	5	123	6	$18,000
21	1	2	2	1	124	6	$18,000
22	1	2	1	3	142	6	$18,000
27	1	1	2	6	125	6	$19,000
28	1	1	3	4	126	6	$19,000
34	2	1	2	2	121	6	$20,000
35 Config 1	1	3	1	1	122	6	$20,000
36	1	1	4	3	124	6	$20,000
37	1	1	2	7	126	6	$20,000
38	1	1	3	5	128	6	$20,000
39	1	2	3	1	130	6	$20,000
29	1	2	1	4	148	5	$19,000
30	1	2	2	2	153	5	$19,000
40	1	2	1	5	151	5	$20,000
41 Config 2	1	2	2	3	166	5	$20,000

This is misleading since the temptation will be to save the $1,000 if both systems will fail five times. The reader should note that the systems are expected to fail five times *on average*, therefore, MTTF hours should not be sacrificed to cost because of number of failures.

Reliability to Reliability of Profit

The example of configuring for reliability can be considered a configuration problem for the engineer. The best that the engineer can accomplish has been described. Additional information was required to form a business context around the problem. The "new" question became, "How much is reliability worth to the business?"

The cost of each system failure, in terms of lost production, is one full day's production or 96 units. If these units are priced at $30, this translates to a cost (lost profit)[44] of $2,880 for each system failure. The base configuration fails nine times per month, reducing profits by $25,920. Configuration 1 reduces this failure rate to six times per month at a cost of $17,280 — a $8,640 improvement! Configuration 2 improves reliability by an additional failure reduction and a $2,880 profit improvement over Configuration 1.

The table below lists the output calculations of the profit model used in the example. The bottom four lines are most interesting. A six month period and twelve month profit differential from Configuration 2 are shown versus the starting "base."

The cumulative difference is $44,160 from "choosing" the proper configuration.

---

[44]   Strictly speaking this is lost revenue, but since our XYZ model does not consider variable cost (i.e., incremental additional cost as each output unit is produced), revenue equals profit in this case.

B-20

In this scenario one might conclude that the "information" leading to the configuration plus the business context information were profit-wise valuable.

	months	1	2	3	4	5	6	12
	hours	720	1440	2160	2880	3600	4320	8640
	Max Revenue	$87,600	$175,200	$262,800	$350,400	$438,000	$525,600	$1,051,200
# of failures	base	9	18	27	36	45	54	108
	config1	6	12	18	24	30	36	72
	config2	5	10	15	20	25	30	60
total cost	base	$12,000	$24,000	$36,000	$48,000	$60,000	$72,000	$144,000
	config1	$20,000	$40,000	$60,000	$80,000	$100,000	$120,000	$240,000
	config2	$20,000	$40,000	$60,000	$80,000	$100,000	$120,000	$240,000
lost profit	base	$26,280	$52,560	$78,840	$105,120	$131,400	$157,680	$315,360
due to failures	config1	$17,520	$35,040	$52,560	$70,080	$87,600	$105,120	$210,240
	config2	$14,600	$29,200	$43,800	$58,400	$73,000	$87,600	$175,200
profit	base	$49,320	$98,640	$147,960	$197,280	$246,600	$295,920	$591,840
	config1	$50,080	$100,160	$150,240	$200,320	$250,400	$300,480	$600,960
	config2	$53,000	$106,000	$159,000	$212,000	$265,000	$318,000	$636,000
cumulative profit	cfg2 over base	$3,680	$7,360	$11,040	$14,720	$18,400	$22,080	$44,160

It is not a stretch to consider the possibility of configuring the enterprise profitability. This might be termed profit engineering.

What is immediately possible is the determination of the degree of profit valuable information that an enterprise exhibits.

If there is not a system-wide metric upon which to judge improvement, the feedback information conduit is missing or broken. In either case, the consequence is likely to be an inferior Return on the Investment. The example has shown that the $8,000 investment has a different return depending on the approach focus.

Information is the key. For without information, the bias is to do nothing. If information is absent, it is easier to continue with the existing system than to increase costs without knowing if the system will improve. Compelling (not costly) information is required to 1) cause investment action and 2) balance the conflicting criteria toward optimization.

The business impact will be necessary at the next meeting also.

	Maximum Revenue (+)	Lost Revenue Due to Failures (-)	System Cost (-)	Monthly Profit =
Base	$86,400	$25,920	$12,000	$48,480
Configuration 2	$86,400	$14,400	$20,000	$52,000

B.3   Information Content Measure Example

We will step through the quantification of the amount of information
content gained in the reliability
position of the example.

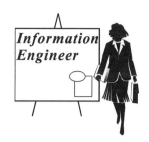

Goal

The goal in this section is the application of the technique
which quantifies the degree of difference of information content relating to the reliability improvement process.

Subject Process Boundaries

The XYZ company reliability improvement process is the
object to which the measure is applied. The goal of that process was the single choice among multiple choices of a
configuration which would improve (maximize) reliability
within constraints of physical, monetary, emotional and other
limitations.

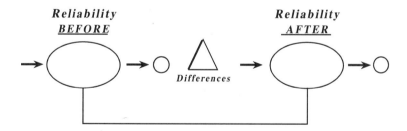

The goal is to measure the difference in the information content
between the before and after.

Calculation of the Natural Solution

The first steps in the calculation consider determination of the natural equilibrium condition.

1.   *Uniform, discrete model choice*
     The model which is appropriate for this case is the discrete form.

$$S = - \Sigma \; P_i \; log \; P_i$$

The basis for this choice is that the physical units of difference (configuration differences) are not fractional. (Note: All "log" calculations are to base 2 throughout this example.)

2.   *Choice set*
     The worst case natural condition is the case where each of the multiple (41) choices are known but cannot be distinguished one from the other. Each choice therefore has the same blind chance of selection.

$$P_i \; = \; 1/41 \; = \; .024$$

The Choice Table shown next is the basis for establishing the minimum (worst) information, highest entropy scale. It is not particularly ordered and the calculations result from the expected value of a blend (uninformed) selections of a configuration.

Choice Table

Choice #	Stage 1	Stage 2	Stage 3	Stage 4
1 (Base)	1	1	1	1
2	1	1	1	2
3	1	1	2	1
4	1	1	1	3
5	1	1	1	4
6	1	1	2	2
7	1	1	3	1
8	1	1	1	5
9	1	2	1	1
10	1	1	2	3
11	2	1	1	1
12	1	1	1	6
13	1	1	3	2
14	1	1	2	4
15	1	2	1	2
16	1	1	4	1
17	2	1	1	2
18	1	1	1	7
19	1	1	3	3
20	1	1	2	5
21	1	2	2	1
22	1	2	1	3
23	2	1	2	1
24	1	1	1	8
25	2	1	1	3
26	1	1	4	2
27	1	1	2	6
28	1	1	3	4
29	1	2	1	4
30	1	2	2	2
31	1	1	5	1
32	1	1	1	9
33	2	1	1	4
34	2	1	2	2
35	1	3	1	1
36	1	1	4	3
37	1	1	2	7
38	1	1	3	5
39	1	2	3	1
40	1	2	1	5
41	1	2	2	3

Choose the best.

3.   *The minimum information calculation*
       The quantification of the scale upon which to form the
       basis is then calculated from the "Choice Table."

$$S = 5.36 \text{ (an information expression)}$$
$$MTTF = 118 \text{ (a reliability expression)}$$
$$\sigma = 16.9 \text{ (a control expression)}$$

This is the basis of the scale from which we will
measure information and reliability gain associative
differences. The reader will note the similarity to
the red, white, blue balls scenario. The condition
where dollars are used as a constraint is no more
meaningful than any other constraint. The only thing
that happened was the change in the number of choices.

4.   *Structure as order*
       The actual (reality) case for the situation next needs to
       be ordered on the basis of goal. This ordering is an
       information process with the output goal of an ordered
       list based on reliability of the 41 choices. Were
       reliability the singular goal criterion then the result
       would have clearly been the 166 MTTF choice.

unit cost =	$5,000	$4,000	$2,000	$1,000		prod.hrs =	720
MTTF =	667	200	500	333		(monthly)	
Choice #	**Stage 1**	**Stage 2**	**Stage 3**	**Stage 4**	**MTTF**	**Cost**	**MTTF/$**
1 (Base)	1	1	1	1	86	$12,000	0.007167
2	1	1	1	2	99	$13,000	0.007615
3	1	1	2	1	95	$14,000	0.006786
4	1	1	1	3	105	$14,000	0.0075
5	1	1	1	4	108	$15,000	0.0072
6	1	1	2	2	111	$15,000	0.0074
7	1	1	3	1	98	$16,000	0.006125
8	1	1	1	5	109	$16,000	0.006813
9	1	2	1	1	111	$16,000	0.006938
10	1	1	2	3	117	$16,000	0.007313
11	2	1	1	1	93	$17,000	0.005471
12	1	1	1	6	111	$17,000	0.006529
13	1	1	3	2	115	$17,000	0.006765
14	1	1	2	4	121	$17,000	0.007118
15	1	2	1	2	133	$17,000	0.007824
16	1	1	4	1	99	$18,000	0.0055
17	2	1	1	2	108	$18,000	0.006
18	1	1	1	7	112	$18,000	0.006222
19	1	1	3	3	122	$18,000	0.006778
20	1	1	2	5	123	$18,000	0.006833
21	1	2	2	1	124	$18,000	0.006889
22	1	2	1	3	142	$18,000	0.007889
23	2	1	2	1	102	$19,000	0.005368
24	1	1	1	8	112	$19,000	0.005895
25	2	1	1	3	114	$19,000	0.006
26	1	1	4	2	117	$19,000	0.006158
27	1	1	2	6	125	$19,000	0.006579
28	1	1	3	4	126	$19,000	0.006632
29	1	2	1	4	148	$19,000	0.007789
30	1	2	2	2	153	$19,000	0.008053
31	1	1	5	1	100	$20,000	0.005
32	1	1	1	9	113	$20,000	0.00565
33	2	1	1	4	117	$20,000	0.00585
34	2	1	2	2	121	$20,000	0.00605
35 **Config 1**	1	3	1	1	122	$20,000	0.0061
36	1	1	4	3	124	$20,000	0.0062
37	1	1	2	7	126	$20,000	0.0063
38	1	1	3	5	128	$20,000	0.0064
39	1	2	3	1	130	$20,000	0.0065
40	1	2	1	5	151	$20,000	0.00755
41 **Config 2**	1	2	2	3	166	$20,000	0.0083

The amount of difference that information difference made to reliability would then be:

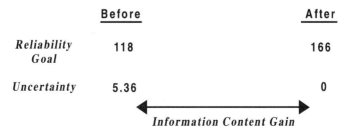

	Before	**After**
Reliability Goal	**118**	**166**
Uncertainty	**5.36**	**0**

Information Content Gain

A blind choice from the list of possible configurations results in an entropy of 5.36 and an average mean time to failure of 118 hours. Notice that a random choice is better than the base case (MTTF = 87). "The amount of difference on an information scale was 5.36. This equated to $5,760 positive difference in revenue and $3,760 positive difference in profitability. That was what the information was worth." Refer to the association diagram below.

The five units of information had the consequence in choosing a configuration that positively deviated 48 MTTF hours from least reliable of the set.

Perspective Note: The author, JT, worked for a period of time with Motorola in the origins of cellular telephony. In that system (as is common in communications), the design goal for reliability was "less than one system failure in 40 years." The MTTF must be greater than 350,640 hours.

5.   *Financial association*
The associative quantification in the change of scale to financial terms can then be exposed in terms of related goal achievement measures. In the case here cost, revenue and profit are commonly related goals.

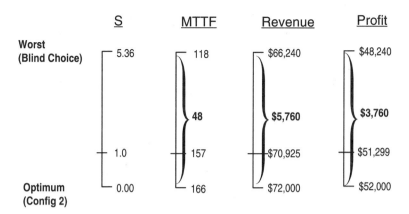

1 unit of information = 9 hrs (MTTF)
1 unit of information = $1,075 (Revenue)
1 unit of information = $701 (Profit)

There is an absence of criteria on exactly which method might be appropriate for quantifying the economic value. A reasonable method that tends to best satisfy the accounting personality is the recreation of history. That is, calculate how <u>much</u> benefit would have accrued last time period (year).

In our case here, we projected forward in time to next year. A debate is likely in either case.

Base Case Explanation

The question arises as to why the base case is not the reference point. First, if base case is used, then the scale is meaningless and destroyed because there is no fundamental constant from which to measure.

Base case here is invalid because the original goal of choice was cost. There was little or no information in evidence of a reliability goal. A blind choice would have yielded higher reliability (review the topic ignorance section). A form of "bonus" occurred because there actually was below zero reliability content in the base minimum cost case.

Unfortunately for XYZ, revenue and profit were dependent on information about reliability. Until XYZ personnel could see the impact, the information was invisible.

When the uncertainty in reliability was reduced by 5.36 units, the associated profit of the enterprise was increased as a consequence.

B.4   *Information about Price Relationships*

The reader is encouraged to briefly
review the section on Bridge (page
121). The information engineer and
the value engineer team together here.
From the earlier discussion appreciate
that price is a pure information object.[45] The entire content is information oriented.

The output goal for the pricing process
is the reduction in uncertainty of which
price or price structure most directly
matches customer value criteria.

The customer value criteria are assumed to be comprised of both functional utility and emotional utility in
the desire for and use of XYZ's offerings.

Choices

The information engineer starts first. Here are the choices.
The current price is $30. We need to acquire information about
a range of price possibilities. Consider the range of possibilities from $15 through $45. This is a thirty-one (31) point
range.

Next consider the combinatorial choices for a pricing structure
that includes a structure of one price, two tier price, three tier
price, four tier price and five tier price.

---

[45]   Also review <u>The Information Advantage</u>, Appendix VII, Pricing, for a more thorough
discussion.

Price Structure	Number of Choices	S
1 Single	31 Combinations	5
2 Tier	465 Combinations	8.9
3 Tier	4,495 Combinations	12.1
4 Tier	31,465 Combinations	14.9
5 Tier	169,911 Combinations	17.4
Total	206,367	17.7

This previous scenario and calculation is offered as an invalid construct. Efficiency of the information engineer synthesis might be the point but in general nothing related to the problem is being measured. This construct is also not the natural case of the situation. Recall the helpful rule that the energy must come from or be about the object being measured.

Moving to Outcomes

The value engineer and the information engineer put their heads together and focus on the outcomes rather than the choices above.

The outcome of the process is going to be 1, 2, 3, 4 or 5 tiered prices. Moreover, if there is more than one price, each will need to be several dollars apart (say 5) one from the other. What will it take to resolve the uncertainty?

Given that the XYZ enterprise chooses to sustain existence, the break-even case aiming is when price equals cost. This is the equilibrium condition from which forms the information quantification basis in this case.

To this point it was not required that "cost" be known. The discussion has been one of incremental difference to some unknown cost base (the reason for such high profits). Consider here that the base cost per unit is known and equal to $6.95.

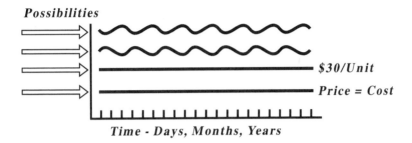

Possibilities

$30/Unit

Price = Cost

Time - Days, Months, Years

An equilibrium case (not good) is where price equals cost. This is a rather continuous process. There may be variation in cost and thus in price but for our purposes here the cost variance is minimal.

The $30 price established at the outset of the example possesses positive information content to the degree that it varies from something worse.

Simultaneously and for each and every transaction during the term, the uncertainty (information deficiency) is exhibited by the evidence of inadaptability to real but unknown possibilities. The absence of action is sufficient evidence of information absence if the goal is sought in a compelling manner.

If this is not the case, the goal is improperly or incompletely defined, else, the information is missing by definition. All this will take is a resolution instrument to determine the match with prospective customer preferences. Here is what the engineers decide to do.

GO ASK!!!

If XYZ properly queries prospective customers then only
several conditions can lead to multiple prices.

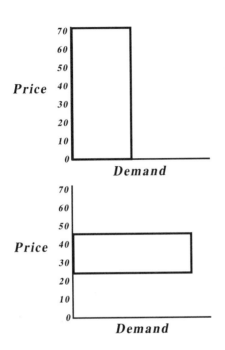

For example, if the price
is found to be concen-
trated in a narrow distribution range as shown in
the top diagram, then
multiple prices will not
be effective. If, however,
the distribution is wide
then the possibility of
tiered pricing is more
likely.

The best practice in a
wide distribution is to let
the customers choose
their own price. You can
see that any price we
choose is wrong. The
implementation vehicle
for "name your own price" is a form of auction. The value
engineer does not see that as a possibility here because of
product and distribution channel constraints.

XYZ has no data from the market and therefore we must design
a factors analysis system to determine the width of the distribution and the possible differentiating ingredients if there is a
meaningful price span. (This was accomplished. Refer to The
Information Advantage, pp. 247-259 or other appropriate
market test tools.)

The collected data are shown below as the frequency distribution of a 500 person market sample. Actually, more than 500 were queried but the distribution below $15 was discarded as not interesting because XYZ made the choice that $15 would be the lowest offering price. Therefore, the 500 units in the distribution relate to those prospects who expressed an appreciation for a price between the limits of $15 and $45.

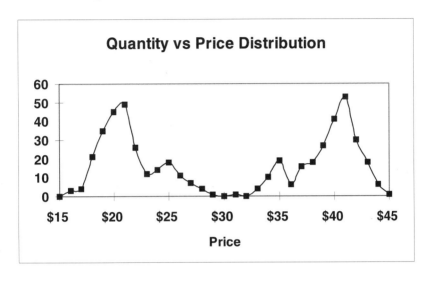

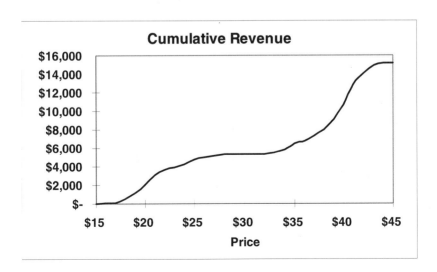

It is unusual to be able to gain the <u>information</u> as to the differentiating factors with a single demographic probe. Constant, repetitive
information about value is required. For illustration purposes
consider that the subtle criteria was "freshness" as in time of day or
time from origination. The value engineer discovered this by
ordering the observation data based on the time stamp of the
collection. It was thus determined that the price powering common
denominator was time. Regardless of the people or stations in life,
the XYZ offering was appreciated in differing degrees at different
times.

Given the appreciation curve, the choice of the pricing structure
is a matter of choosing the configuration that creates goal
gains. The reader may note a similarity to reliability.

The value engineer, being quite certain of the integrity of the
sample, applied various models to gather the area (revenue).
There is no magic here. For illustration purposes four (4)
candidates are shown on the next diagram. (Note that two tier
and three tier price curves overlap.)

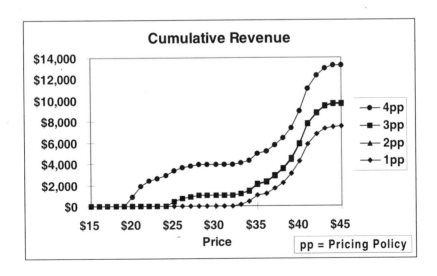

The cumulative review (for 500 units) is shown for the following policies:

 a) Single ($30)
 b) Two tier price ($25, $35)
 c) Three tier price ($25, $30, $35)
 d) Four tier price ($20, $25, $35, $45)

The next task for the value engineer was the transfer of the policy to the actual production situation of XYZ (96 units/day).

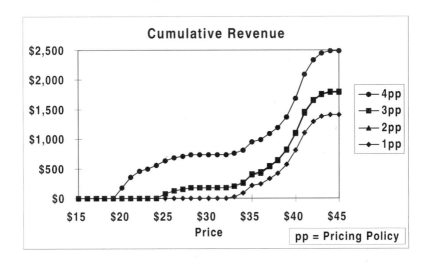

The price configuration recommended is as follows:

First 20 each day	$40/unit
Next 30 each day	$35/unit
Next 30 each day	$25/unit
Remainder each day	$20/unit

The consequence on monthly revenue and profit is:

	Before	After
Revenue	72,000	73,000
Profit	52,000	53,000

B.5   *Information Content Calculation - Example*

The reliability example of information content was primarily internal production focused. The information content was construction oriented and then associated outward. In the pricing content, the reverse flow occurs. The information content exists outbound and flows inward.

Price is strictly an analysis of the "aiming" process in the same sense as that of the archer (page 107). Nothing particularly changed in the manufacturing, construction or cost structure of XYZ. The only thing that was altered was the effectiveness.

The information content is determined as follows.

Natural Equilibrium Basis

The goal in pricing process is the matching of offering price to customer appreciation. Any deviations in the match causes sub-goal effectiveness.

Basis Calculation

Two information content scenarios will be presented for purposes of illustration. The authors believe it will help to show the method using the "sample" 500 unit distribution and then show again the XYZ application scenario which recomputes the content. We hope to show by accomplishing this dual scenario more exactly where the information content differs. Caution — we have found that it is the "thinking" about the problem which is the most difficult.

500 Unit Sample Information Content

Consider that the frequency distribution previously described is a profile of customer appreciation for the XYZ company offering. It is most exactly that.

Deming called this the "voice of the customer." In this case it is the voice of 500 customers for a very similar offering.

There is no possible way for a single fixed price (i.e., $30) to "match" a distribution of mixed value appreciation.

The maximum information content in such a system would be the choice to exactly (invariably) price each unit sold to match the individual customer appreciation.

The inability to control this goal is the measure of the missing information (the uncertainty).

For the sample in question, we will establish the equilibrium condition by equating cost of construction to offering price.

The cumulative revenue would then be 500 units times the $6.95 price. (Yes, we know we excluded perhaps many in the throwing away of the prospects below $15. For convenience, ignore these.)

We will add this option to the cumulative price/revenue distribution shown earlier.

Secondly, we know that the maximum information for this situation would result in price exactly matching appreciation. This will be the zero uncertainty case (S=0).

The following diagram includes the two additional cumulative revenue distributions along with those previously presented from the value engineer.

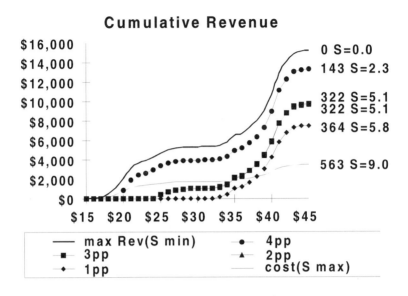

Cumulative Revenue

Using the same calculations as presented in the "archer," we can calculate the variance from (in this case) best. The variance calculations are now attributed to the corresponding price policy and consequential revenue.

Pricing Policy	Relative Distance From Best	
Exact Match	0	Perfect Information
4 Tier Price Structure	143	
3 Tier Price Structure	322	
2 Tier Price Structure	322	
Single $30	364	
Single $6.95	563	Worst Case Uncertainty

The variances are directly linked to uncertainty in the Boltzman formula and thus the corresponding information content measures are shown in association.

Pricing Policy	Variance Measure	(Uncertainty) Information Content	Revenue Consequence
Exact Match	0	0	$ 15207
4 Tier Price Structure	143	2.3	$ 13290
3 Tier Price Structure	322	5.1	$ 9700
2 Tier Price Structure	322	5.1	$ 9625
Single $30	364	5.8	$ 7500
Single $6.95	563	9	$ 3475

As such the value of resolving the uncertainty is measurable and calculable and determines the value of the information and/ or the cost of uncertainty.

Second Scenario - XYZ Case Example

XYZ company does not manufacture 500 units. Rather it manufactures 96 units per period of time where the price is appropriate (daily). XYZ has less uncertainty in its system by virtue of only having 96 choices to make before the process is reset (repeated).

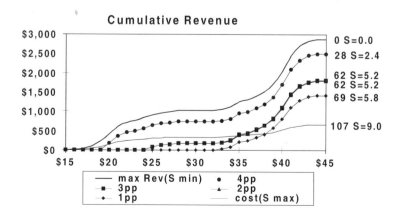

The profile is the same but the situation setting is altered relative to the 500 choice scenario.

Applying the identical technique to the XYZ situation results in the following corresponding information content analysis:

Pricing Policy	Variance Measure	(Uncertainty) Information Content	Revenue Consequence
Exact Match	0	0	$ 2,869
4 Tier Price Structure	28	2.4	$ 2,490
3 Tier Price Structure	62	5.2	$ 1,805
2 Tier Price Structure	62	5.2	$ 1,790
Single $30	69	5.8	$ 1,410
Single $6.95	107	9	$ 660

Index

J. D. Thoreson

Mr. Thoreson, "JT," earned a Bachelor of Science degree in Mechanical Engineering and a Master of Science degree in Industrial and Management Engineering (Operations Research) from the State University of Iowa. His professional career is best characterized as an impressive series of successful innovation "firsts" in applied large-scale systems engineering integration. Notable intellectual work includes pioneering group thoughtware technologies, display thinking and spatial visualization. He has submitted for patents method, technique and apparatus for generalized information value determination. Conventional and innovative commercial applications include microwave cooking, clad metal coinmaking, cellular telephony, manufacturing engineering automation, distributed computing, desktop microprocessors, factory floor controllers, artificial intelligence and neural networks. Successful industry applications include manufacturing, public utilities, communications, life insurance and transportation. Mr. Thoreson founded and managed consulting companies and participated in the health care team that captured the claims processing marketplace.

John H. Blankenship

Dr. Blankenship earned a Bachelor of Science degree in Mathematics, a Master of Science degree in Mathematical Statistics, and a Doctor of Philosophy in Mathematics and Statistics from Oklahoma State University. Dr. Blankenship is a recognized international authority in the top disciplines of applied operations research and management science techniques, switched communications networks, interactive graphics, and computer automated manufacturing (CAM) including robotics, nesting, materials handling and communications. Dr. Blankenship has had responsibility for the management of software research and development; creation of major CAM systems; creation of widely used banking software tools; hardware and software support and specification development for various large scale distributed application systems. He also has consulted in such areas as applied operations research, automated voting, mathematical analysis of circuits and high reliability communications systems. He has served as a principal and partner, as well as founder, to Dallas-based consulting corporations.